I Dissent

I Dissent

Great Opposing Opinions in Landmark Supreme Court Cases

EDITED BY

MARK TUSHNET

BEACON PRESS, BOSTON

Beacon Press
25 Beacon Street
Boston, Massachusetts 02108-2892
www.beacon.org

Beacon Press books
are published under the auspices of
the Unitarian Universalist Association of Congregations.

11 10 09 08   8 7 6 5 4 3 2 1

This book is printed on acid-free paper that meets the uncoated paper
ANSI/NISO specifications for permanence as revised in 1992.

Text design and composition by Susan E. Kelly
at Wilsted & Taylor Publishing Services

Library of Congress Cataloging-in-Publication Data

I dissent : great opposing opinions in landmark Supreme Court cases / edited
by Mark Tushnet.
    p. cm.
    ISBN 978-0-8070-0036-6
    1. United States. Supreme Court—History. 2. Judicial opinions—United
States—Cases. 3. Judicial review—United States—Cases. 4. Constitutional
law—United States—Cases. I. Tushnet, Mark V.

KF8742.135 2008
347.73'2609—dc22   2007031511

For Nora Emily

CONTENTS

Why Dissent?

Our constitutional tradition celebrates the great dissenters—
John Marshall Harlan, Oliver Wendell Holmes, William O.
Douglas. On one level, the reason is clear: out of step with the
prevailing constitutional views of their times, they were vindicated by history. The nation came to see the wisdom of *their*
constitutional views, and the errors of the majorities that temporarily prevailed.

That is a comforting story—except for the fact that there
are *always* dissenters, and we never know which is going to be
vindicated and which repudiated by history. Once we realize, as
we must, that some dissenters were wrong at the moment they
dissented and wrong thereafter, the story about dissent, and
about how history decides who is the winner and who the loser,
becomes much more complicated.

I think it useful to begin by laying out some reasons for being skeptical about the very idea of a dissenting opinion. Imagine that you are justice on the Supreme Court. You have read
the briefs and heard the arguments made in a case, and you
have discussed the case with the other justices, who of course
have examined exactly the same materials. You think that,
properly read and interpreted, the Constitution requires that
the plaintiff win her case. Five, six, even eight of your colleagues
disagree. They read the legal materials to require that the plain-

tiff lose. You have done your best to show them that they are wrong, but they remain adamant. The opinion of the Court is issued, holding for the defendant.

We are accustomed to thinking that you should—or at least can—dissent, explaining your reasons for disagreeing with your colleagues. Yet, a skeptic might think, isn't publishing a dissent a self-indulgent, largely pointless, and possibly damaging act? After all, you and your colleagues have all examined the same materials. Why should you think that your take on the law is better than the considered views of your colleagues? Of course, if you thought that they were less capable than you, or had failed to do as conscientious a job as you, you might well reject their conclusions—but then aren't you being a bit arrogant?

And, in the end, what do you accomplish by publishing a dissent? Your views have lost out. The plaintiff is going to walk away without a remedy no matter what you do. The law will be as the majority declares it to be, and courts in the future will look to the majority opinion, not to yours, for guidance on the Constitution's meaning. You might hope that something you say in your dissent—"It's a good thing that the majority limits its decision to the facts of this case," for example—might lead lower court judges to interpret the majority opinion as you hope they will. But the majority opinion is there for everyone to read, and a judge who wants to read it in a limiting way can do so without your guidance (and a judge who wants to read it expansively isn't going to listen to you).

You may feel that publishing a dissent shows that you put up a good fight but lost in the end, but all that means is that you get to feel a little bit better about yourself, and may signal to people whose approval you seek that you are with them. And, after all, you get to feel better even as the plaintiff ends up worse off. It would not be hard to describe this as an unattractive way of salving your own conscience while neglecting the person who really lost the case. Sometimes, of course, you might think that affirmatively signing on to the majority's decision would amount to cooperation with evil. That might justify a notation, "Justice X dissents," but not a full-fledged dissenting opinion. (Maybe law clerks today won't let a justice get away with something so simple, and it's easy enough to tell a law clerk to draft a dissent.)

Even more, publishing a dissent might be damaging to the law itself. The continental legal tradition is so concerned about this prospect that some European nations have made it a crime for a judge to publish a dissent or even to make it known, through conversations or private letters, that she disagreed with one of her court's decisions. The reason is that the mere existence of a published dissent will give some people—those who agree with the losing side, for example—one reason to hold on to their belief about what the law really is. And, holding *that* belief, they might act on it. Suppose the decision says that it is unconstitutional to hold a U.S. citizen as an "enemy combatant" based on secret evidence unless the government makes a strong showing that disclosing the evidence would harm the war effort. You dissent, saying that the government's assertion that disclosing the evidence would harm the war effort should be enough. Your dissent might encourage government officials to continue to hold someone based on flimsy evidence of damage from disclosing secret evidence. They might hope that your dissent will signal to lower court judges that they do not have to be too stringent in applying the majority's "strong evidence" rule, or they might hope that when the case comes to your court, you yourself will apply that rule in a pro-government way.

The concern that published dissents weaken the rule of law has even more bite where the courts need support from both government officials and ordinary people to ensure that the courts' decisions are actually implemented. The classic example is school segregation (discussed in Chapter 11). Chief Justice Earl Warren and his colleagues whose legal analysis led them to conclude that segregation was unconstitutional worried that a dissent would provide the decision's opponents—and they knew that there would be many opponents—with ammunition to charge the Court with acting contrary to law. That worry is deepened when, as often happens, the dissent itself makes that charge, sometimes implicitly through its own legal analysis, and sometimes explicitly through statements that the majority's decision can be explained not by legal analysis but only by the majority's personal preferences.

Still, you might think that weakening the rule of law in this way would be a good thing. After all, you think that the majority's decision is wrong, perhaps evenly deeply wrong, as a matter of law. Making it less likely that the decision will "stick" is desirable from your point of view. Maybe so, but it is probably worth noting that, when the stakes are not all that high, the harm a dissent does to the idea that judges are simply interpreting the law and not implementing their policy preferences might often outweigh the self-satisfaction you get from explaining why you are right and your colleagues are wrong. (It is a real puzzle to understand why judges publish long and detailed dissents from decisions interpreting obscure provisions of the federal tax or pension laws, for example.)

Even when the stakes are high, you might not get more than self-satisfaction out of dissenting. Consider a case in which your analysis of the First Amendment's protection of freedom of speech leads you to conclude that it is unconstitutional to send someone to jail for criticizing the government's policy in vigorous terms, and your colleagues' analysis leads them to conclude that convictions for that offense are perfectly constitutional (for an example, see Chapter 7). Suppose a bunch of people agree with you and act on that belief by making exactly the kinds of speech that led to imprisonment in the case you decided. What's going to happen to them? In the short run—as long as you continue to be outvoted by your colleagues—they are going to prison.

Maybe, though, the people who agree with your dissent will not make *exactly* the same speeches that got others into trouble. Their criticisms of the government, as lawyers would put it, are distinguishable from the ones your colleagues held to be punishable. Your dissent might encourage prosecutors and lower court judges to think twice about "extending" the Court's decision to this new situation.

All this buys into a complicated and probably mistaken "theory" about how one case serves as a precedent for another. To continue with the example: Last year your colleagues upheld a conviction for criticizing the government, and you dissented. This year another case involving a similar but slightly different speech comes back to the Court. What are the possibilities?

- Your colleagues think that the same principle that justified the conviction last year justifies a conviction this year. Your dissent has no effect on the outcome.

- Your colleagues think that last year's principle does *not* extend to cover this year's speech, and they let the speaker off. Again, your dissent has no effect.

And what about you?

- You still think that last year's decision was wrong, and you stick by your guns. Whether this year's speech is distinguishable doesn't matter to you.

- You still think that last year's decision was wrong, but you think that, even applying the majority's erroneous principle, the speech is constitutionally protected, and you vote to let the speaker off. It is probably worth observing that your colleagues may think to themselves that your willingness to distinguish this case from last year's is a bit convenient, especially if *they* think that their principle, properly applied, means that this year's defendant should go to jail, too.

So far, the fact that you dissented in the first case does not have any effects on the second. There are a couple of other possibilities, though.

- Your dissent last year might have eaten away at your colleagues' commitments, and some of them will change their minds, join you, and vote to overrule the decision they made last year. This is possible, and does happen. But it should be no surprise that it does not happen often. After all, the reasons you gave last year did not persuade them then, and—unless something new has happened (an important qualification)—it is hard to see why those very same reasons should suddenly persuade them now.

- You might say to yourself that you have a duty to apply the entire body of law, including last year's precedent, and that, when you do so, this year's speech is covered by the Court's (erroneous) principle. So, you vote to send the speaker to jail. This too happens, but again rarely, for the obvious reason: you think that, if your colleagues had gotten the law right last year, this defendant would go free, but because they made a mistake last year, she has to go to jail. This is not going to be a comfortable decision for you to make, and as long as there is some possible way of distinguishing this year's case from last year's, you are going to be strongly tempted to say that the cases are different even under your colleagues' principle.

The conclusion of all this is that your dissent is not going to have much effect on outcomes in the short run. It is not going to keep your colleagues from extending their mistaken decision, although they might refrain from repeating their logic in this new case for their own reasons.

A large part of the reason, though, is that you are dealing with the same colleagues who made a mistake when they decided the first case. Change the players, and the outcomes might change. And, after all, if you wrote your dissent "for history," your assumption is that someday the players will change — that is, that there will be new justices on the Supreme Court who might share your constitutional vision.

At this point, saying that your dissent matters becomes quite tricky. Simplifying only a bit: new justices who share your constitutional vision get appointed when there is a new president who does the same. And how does that happen? Mostly, for reasons unconnected to your dissent, or indeed to the Supreme Court as a whole. An economic depression, a popular or unpopular war, demographic changes, migration from one part of the nation to another—all these are usually far more important in determining who the president is than what the Supreme Court does.

Usually, but not always. Occasionally, a presidential candidate may find it strategically useful to run against the Court, as Richard Nixon did in campaigning as a "law and order" candidate whose Supreme Court appointments would reverse the liberal criminal procedure precedents of the Warren Court. Such a candidate might build dissents from within the Court into the standard stump speech. Even in these campaigns, though, the candidate's victory or defeat rarely turns on the issue of the Supreme Court: in the 1990s and after, Democrats routinely tried and failed to scare pro-choice voters into voting against Republican candidates who, if elected, would appoint justices who would in turn overrule *Roe v. Wade.*

Yet, sometimes what I have referred to as *constitutional visions* do matter in elections. Candidates run on platforms that implicate constitutional values: equality, domestic and international security, social justice. These platforms occasionally refer to Supreme Court decisions. In 1860 the Republican Party's platform denounced "the new dogma, that the Constitution, of its own force, carries Slavery into any or all of the Territories of the United States," as "a dangerous political heresy," alluding to the Supreme Court's decision in the Dred Scott case (Chapter 3), and modern political platforms have regularly taken positions on *Roe v. Wade.* More important, though, the platforms are infused with more general ideas about the way the political party's candidates think the Constitution should be implemented.

Those ideas come mostly from the party's political supporters, and in particular from the social movements that influence the general shape of American political parties. The civil rights movement of the 1960s produced a constitutional vision of racial and social equality that worked its way into the Democratic Party's platforms; the Christian Right developed a competing constitutional vision that was embodied in Republican platforms at the end of the twentieth century and after. Supreme Court decisions made some modest contributions to these social-movement visions. Urging Montgomery's African Americans to support the ongoing boycott of their city's segregated bus system in 1955, Martin Luther King Jr. said, "We are not wrong. If we are wrong, the Supreme Court of this nation is wrong. If we are wrong, the Constitution of the United States is wrong. If we are wrong, God Almighty is wrong." The social conservatism of the Christian Right reacted against *Roe v. Wade* and the Court's decisions on school prayer (see Chapter 13). Scholars outside the legal academy who study these movements believe, though, that the Supreme Court's contributions to the construction and appeal of these general constitutional visions are smaller than lawyers think they are (or hope them to be). King's speech only began with a reference to the Supreme Court; it culminated with a reference to God Almighty.

Constitutional visions do matter to the Supreme Court—because presidents whose campaigns include appeals to such visions sometimes nominate Supreme Court justices who share their visions. Again, some historical perspective can deflate the importance of constitutional visions in the nomination process. The politics of judicial nominations mirrors politics generally. When ordinary politics involves interest-group bargaining, so does the politics of judicial nominations. That was true for most of the period from the 1870s to the 1950s. William O. Douglas was nominated to the Supreme Court in 1939 because he was from the West (and was a reliable New Dealer on economic questions), not because he was a strong civil libertarian. Some judicial appointments are straightforward political payoffs. The most important of these in recent history was the nomination of Earl Warren as chief justice in 1954 (see Chapter 11). And, importantly, when constitutional visions matter in politics generally, they will matter in judicial nominations. That was true with respect to constitutional visions about economic regulation during the New Deal, and it is true today: when presidents and senators inquire into what they call a person's "judicial philosophy" (if they like the person) or "judicial ideology" (if they do not), they are really asking about the person's constitutional vision.

So, dissents can matter, but in quite an indirect way: a dissent *might* be picked up by a social movement because the dissent expresses something the movement already has in its constitutional vision; the social movement's constitutional vision *might* affect a political party and its candidates; successful candidates *might* nominate judges and justices because of *their* constitutional visions; and these new justices *might* conclude that the dissent—by now, perhaps years in the past—provides a better account of our Constitution than the majority opinion does. All of the qualifications are important here.

That the path from dissent to effects is so indirect also helps illuminate a question we might naturally ask about dissents: how would our world be different had the dissenters prevailed? In one sense, the answer is ordinarily going to be simple: "not much." There almost certainly would have been a Civil War no matter what the Supreme Court said in the Dred Scott case (Chapter 3); African Americans in the South would almost certainly have faced substantial discrimination no matter what the Supreme Court said in the *Civil Rights Cases* (Chapter 4) or *Plessy v. Ferguson* (Chapter 5). And the reason the world would not be much different is simple, too. The way our world looks is determined far more by economics, social change, demographics, and the like than it is by Supreme Court decisions. It takes a long time to traverse the indirect path I described, and during that time lots of other things change. When the dissent is "vindicated," should we explain that result by saying that the decision was right from the start, or by noting all the other things that happened between the time the dissent was written and the time it became the law?

That dissents matter, but almost always indirectly and over a long period, shapes what we can say about recent dissents, and explains why this book includes only a single dissent from the twenty-first century. The more recent the dissent, the harder it is to know what social, economic, and political developments will occur that will lead the dissent to fall by the way-side or to become important.

Perhaps, then, dissents that are "merely" interesting are ones that no important social movements pick up. The great dissenters are those whose dissents resonate with the constitutional visions of the social movements that in the long run have affected our political system.

The dissents compiled here span most of the Supreme Court's history. The collection offers a quick overview of almost all the important issues the Court has dealt with, although of course there are gaps. I introduce each dissent with a short description of the background against which the case was decided—not only its facts, but sometimes its political and social setting. I have edited the dissents, sometimes severely, to make them as accessible as possible to readers who are not lawyers, but I believe that I have preserved enough of the *legal* analysis in each opinion to make it clear that these are dissents from Supreme Court opinions, not editorial essays about the policy or politics of the Court's decision. Each dissent is followed by a discussion of the dissent's effects and significance. I have used these followup discussions to introduce several themes important in today's conversations about constitutional law generally. Among those themes are these:

- *The rhetoric of dissent.* Styles of opinion writing have changed. Older opinions are more ornate than more recent ones. Justice John Marshall Harlan's opinions go on at enormous length, much of which appears, even after editing, to be wheel-spinning that does not advance any discernible argument (for an example, see Chapter 4). Justice Robert Jackson wrote more sparely, and was a master at turning phrases that captured deep insights, but he too sometimes had difficulty in sustaining an argument from beginning to end (for an example, see Chapter II). On the Court today, Justice Antonin Scalia has perfected the "opinion as attack ad" rhetoric, offering quotable criticisms that writers of op ed pieces can incorporate into their work without saying anything new (for an example, see Chapter 16). Of the opinions in this book, Justice Louis Brandeis's dissent in *Whitney v. California* (Chapter 7) is certainly the most elegant freestanding piece of prose—somewhat surprisingly, coming from the pen of someone who might be described as the justice with the soul of an accountant.

• *Great dissenters.* A few judges appear more than once in what follows. Taking account of the fact that my selections embody personal judgments made in an effort to provide selections from the entire history of the Supreme Court dealing with most of the major issues the Court has addressed, we might consider why these judges play a seemingly special role—and why other judges, notably William O. Douglas, who once were regarded as great dissenters, do not appear in the collection. For Justice Douglas, the answer is easy: his dissents *were* vindicated by history, but his writing style was somewhat slapdash and, probably more important, he actually took seriously the legal views against which he was writing. The effect was to make Justice Douglas's dissents curiously time-bound. We might contrast him with Justice John Marshall Harlan, whose writing style seems quite ornate to us today, but whose dissents were animated by a powerful moral vision that retains its appeal. One final note: it is too soon to tell whether Justice Antonin Scalia, who appears twice in this collection, will someday be seen as a great dissenter. We don't know whether his constitutional vision will be vindicated, and—although here I know that I have idiosyncratic views—his writing style, widely admired today, may have less staying power than most people believe it will.

- *Legal doctrine as precedent.* We must interpret dissents to know what they mean, just as we must interpret majority opinions. And, just as with majority opinions, the meaning of a dissent depends at least as much on what *we* choose to make of it as it does on what its author meant. Precedents— and here we are considering dissents as precedents—can be extended in many directions, and their words are typically inadequate to project only one meaning for the future. The most dramatic example in this collection is Justice John Marshall Harlan's dissent in *Plessy v. Ferguson* (Chapter 5). Written at the end of the nineteenth century, the dissent was used in the twenty-first to explain why affirmative ac- tion programs were unconstitutional *and* why they were perfectly constitutional. Importantly, neither side was "mis- using" the dissent. Both pro- and anti-affirmative action themes can fairly be found in the dissent, and Justice Har- lan did not have to choose between them. Both themes pointed to striking down the segregation statute he was dealing with, and he had no reason to worry about prob- lems of affirmative action that were nearly one hundred years in the future.

- *Political change and the vindication of dissents.* Several of the dissents included here have been—or might yet be—vindi- cated by history. Federal antidiscrimination laws held un- constitutional in the *Civil Rights Cases* (Chapter 4) are now uncontroversial, though their formal constitutional foundations are different from the ones found inadequate in those cases. Racial segregation, held constitutional in *Plessy,* is now unconstitutional. Legislative regulation of the wages paid to ordinary workers was held unconstitutional in *Lochner v. New York* (Chapter 6), and is today so obviously constitutional that the only debates we have are over what the federally mandated minimum wage should be, not whether the Constitution allows Congress to prescribe a minimum wage.

Before taking a completely sunny view of these prescient dissents, we should remember that a dissent's vindication, if it comes, is the product of a complex social and political process. Some of the dissents were not vindicated, but the Court's holdings prevailed only after strong resistance was overcome. Seeing how dissents gradually became the law may be one of the best ways of seeing the connections between constitutional law resulting from the interplay of law, economics, politics, and society generally. In such cases we *know* that it was not law alone—or at least not law as laid down by the Supreme Court—that produced the outcomes we see, because these are cases where the law was one thing earlier and exactly the opposite later.

• *Popular constitutionalism.* A final theme introduces one of the more interesting developments in recent constitutional scholarship—the idea of popular constitutionalism. (A disclaimer: at least it is one of the more interesting themes to me, because I have been associated with the revival of interest in popular constitutionalism.)

Popular constitutionalism insists that responsibility for ensuring that our system of government adheres to the basic precepts of our Constitution lies at least as much with the American people as a whole as it does with Supreme Court justices and other judges—and that the judges' views about what the Constitution means have no particularly strong claim on the people, except to the extent that the judges give reasons supporting their interpretations that the people come to agree with.

Popular constitutionalism has been a persistent part of the U.S. constitutional experience. Critics of judicial review, early and late, have questioned why the judges' views about the Constitution should always win out when the judges disagree with the constitutional views embodied in legislation adopted by the people and their representatives. I have included an early opinion critical of judicial review as the "dissent" to the Supreme Court's unanimous decision in *Marbury v. Madison* (Chapter 1) as an illustration. Politicians have regularly asserted their right to disagree with the courts about the Constitution's meaning. As the dissent to the Court's unanimous decision in *McCulloch v. Maryland* (Chapter 2), I have included President Andrew Jackson's message to Congress explaining why he vetoed a statute because he believed it to be unconstitutional even though the Supreme Court had made it clear that, in its view, the statute did not violate the Constitution. (An incidental benefit of including these "dissents" is that they show, concretely, that important discussions of constitutional law occur outside the Supreme Court—in state courts and in presidential messages.)

There is a vigorous debate in the legal academy today over the merits of popular constitutionalism, and I sketch some of the reasons for skepticism about popular constitutionalism in some of the followup discussions of particular dissents. And yet, if the overall argument I have made here is right—that what the Constitution comes to mean results from the way social movements, politics, economics, and more lead us to think about what the Constitution's words mean—perhaps all constitutional law is popular constitutionalism. In which case, reading dissents is as important as reading majority opinions in helping us understand constitutional law.

CHAPTER 1

"The legislature is entitled to all the deference that is due the judiciary."

Marbury v. Madison, 1803

January 1801: Thomas Jefferson's Democratic Party has just won a massive victory in the elections held in November 1800, taking over the presidency and control of both houses of Congress from John Adams and the Federalist Party. But, because of the extended transition period between the election and the new government taking office, the Federalists still had a chance to hold on to some power. They could not do anything about the legislative or executive branches, but the courts were another matter.

Adams and his Federalists decided to pack the courts with their political allies. Sensible proposals for judicial reform had been rattling around for a while. The Federalists decided to implement them. One effect was to give them a chance to appoint a large number of new judges.

The judicial reform legislation created two classes of new judges. The more important ones were lifetime appointments to the major federal courts. The others were minor judicial officials in the District of Columbia. Adams moved quickly to name the judges, and the Senate to confirm them. Then, unfortunately for the Federalists, Secretary of State John Marshall, soon to take his seat as chief justice of the Supreme Court, made a mistake: after President Adams signed the "commissions," the official documents stating that the new judges were indeed entitled to their positions, Marshall let some of them sit on his desk. Some were still sitting there when Thomas Jefferson took office as president.

Jefferson and his party were determined to undo the Federalists' initiatives. They repealed the statute creating the important new judges and tried to insulate their action from review by what they expected to be a hostile Supreme Court by directing that the Court not meet as scheduled in 1801 or 1802. And Jefferson refused to deliver the remaining commissions, including one to William Marbury.

Marbury wanted his office—or at least he wanted to create a political hassle for Jefferson. He filed a claim in the Supreme Court seeking an order directing that James Madison, the new secretary of state, deliver his commission. John Marshall and his Supreme Court colleagues faced a dilemma. They could chastise Jefferson for his "lawless" action in withholding the commission and direct him to give it to Marbury, and they might gain some political points from Federalists for doing so, but Jefferson would almost certainly have ignored their order. Or, they could fold their tents and acknowledge their weak political position by letting Jefferson get away with what Federalists feared would be the first of many dictatorial actions.

Marshall figured out a better course. In his opinion for *Marbury v. Madison,* Marshall spent a great deal of space explaining why Marbury had a legal right to his commission, but then explained why the Supreme Court could not order Jefferson to give it to him in this case. Marbury had filed his claim in the Supreme Court without first attempting to get a lower court to issue an order to Jefferson or Madison. Marshall asked whether there was some statute that gave the Supreme Court the power to issue the order in such an "original" action. He then found such a statute, although scholars ever since have contended with some force that Marshall distorted the statute's language to find the authorization there. Finally, at the very end, the opinion took a sharp turn. Marshall asked whether this statute was consistent with the Constitution. Again developing a reading of the Constitution's terms that few since have found compelling, Marshall found the statute inconsistent with the Constitution. He *said* that Marbury's legal rights had been violated, but he *decided* that Marbury couldn't get a remedy from the Supreme Court.

Marshall's final move was the one of the most enduring significance. Faced with a statute that—as interpreted—violated the Constitution as interpreted, what should the courts do? Marshall said, Ignore the statute. That is, Marshall held that the courts had the duty to refuse to enforce a statute they found unconstitutional.

Jefferson was outraged at the early parts of the opinion, which essentially called him a lawbreaker, but because Marshall had not ordered Jefferson to deliver the commission there was nothing Jefferson could do about it. And when the Court did have to face up to the Federalist challenge to its authority, it gave in and upheld what the Federalists had done. Marshall, it seems, calculated that in the long run the courts would become a powerful institution of government if they declined to confront Jefferson directly, but asserted that they had the *power* to do so in an appropriate case.

The power of judicial review was, in the abstract, not terribly controversial. For the past generation or more, American constitutionalists had assumed that courts did have the power to ignore laws they found inconsistent with the Constitution, although the precise scope of the power was a matter of some minor dispute. Nor was anyone seriously bothered by Marshall's use of the power in *Marbury v. Madison* to invalidate an unimportant, technical statute. But some of Marshall's arguments for judicial review were open to serious question. He said that judges took an oath to support the Constitution, and they could hardly be asked to violate that oath by enforcing an unconstitutional statute. He bolstered that argument by posing some hypotheticals. One was this: the Constitution says that a person can be convicted of treason only if he confesses in open court or if there are two witnesses to the defendant's treasonous actions. Suppose Congress passes a statute saying that a person can be convicted of treason based on the testimony of only one witness. Surely the courts could not send a person to his death after a trial in which only one witness testified as to the treasonous actions.

The problem with Marshall's arguments was that they assumed that everyone knew when a statute violated the Constitution. The treason example was clear because both the imagined statute and the actual constitutional provision were perfectly clear. What, though, of a constitutional provision that was less clear? Members of Congress also took an oath to support the Constitution. When they enact a statute that would be constitutional if the Constitution is read one way and unconstitutional if read differently, shouldn't the courts assume that the members of Congress were conscientious about their oaths and believed that the statute was consistent with the Constitution? Should courts assume that members of Congress believed that the first way was the *right* interpretation of the Constitution? And, if the courts made that assumption, why should it matter that the judges acting on their own would have interpreted the Constitution differently? Marshall's opinion provided no answer to that question.

Marbury v. Madison was a unanimous decision by the U.S. Supreme Court. Two decades later, in *Eakin v. Raub* (1825), Justice John Gibson of the Pennsylvania Supreme Court "dissented" from its holding. Justice Gibson's colleagues held unconstitutional a state statute that extended a statute of limitations, thereby—according to the majority—impermissibly allowing a plaintiff to revive a "dead" claim. Justice Gibson dissented, and took the opportunity to explain why the courts should not have the power to invalidate legislation.

GIBSON, J., dissenting. . . .

[I]n questions of this sort, precedents ought to go for absolutely nothing. The constitution is a collection of fundamental laws, not to be departed from in practice nor altered by judicial decision. . . .

The constitution and the *right* of the legislature to pass the act, may be in collision. But is that a legitimate subject for judicial determination? If it be, the judiciary must be a peculiar organ, to revise the proceedings of the legislature, and to correct its mistakes; and in what part of the constitution are we to look for this proud pre-eminence? Viewing the matter in the opposite direction, what would be thought of an act of assembly in which it should be declared that the Supreme Court had, in a particular case, put a wrong construction on the constitution of the *United States,* and that the judgment should therefore be reversed? It would doubtless be thought a usurpation of judicial power. But it is by no means clear, that to declare a law void which has been enacted according to the forms prescribed in the constitution, is not a usurpation of legislative power. . . . It is the business of the judiciary to interpret the laws, not scan the authority of the lawgiver; and without the latter, it cannot take cognizance of a collision between a law and the constitution. So that to affirm that the judiciary has a right to judge of the existence of such collision is to take for granted the very thing to be proved. . . .

But it has been said to be emphatically the business of the judiciary, to ascertain and pronounce what the law is; and that this necessarily involves a consideration of the constitution. It does so: but how far? If the judiciary will inquire into any thing beside the form of enactment, where shall it stop? There must be some point of limitation to such an inquiry; for no one will pretend, that a judge would be justifiable in calling for the election returns, or scrutinizing the qualifications of those who composed the legislature.

... [L]et it be supposed that the power to declare a law unconstitutional has been exercised. What is to be done? The legislature must acquiesce, although it may think the construction of the judiciary wrong. But why must it acquiesce? Only because it is bound to pay that respect to every other organ of the government, which it has a right to exact from each of them in turn. This is the argument. But it will not be pretended, that the legislature has not at least an equal right with the judiciary to put a construction on the constitution; nor that either of them is infallible; nor that either ought to be required to surrender its judgment to the other. Suppose, then, they differ in opinion as to the constitutionality of a particular law; if the organ whose business it first is to decide on the subject, is not to have its judgment treated with respect, what shall prevent it from securing the preponderance of its opinion by the strong arm of power? It is in vain to say, the legislature would be the aggressor in this; and that no argument in favour of its authority can be drawn from an abuse of its power. Granting this, yet it is fair to infer, that the framers of the constitution never intended to force the judges either to become martyrs or to flinch from their duty; or to interpose a check that would produce no other effect than an intestine war. Such things have occurred in other states, and would necessarily occur in this, under circumstances of strong excitement in the popular branch. The judges would be legislated out of office, if the majority requisite to a direct removal by impeachment, or the legislative address, could not be had; and this check, instead of producing the salutary effect expected from it, would rend the government in pieces. But suppose that a struggle would not produce consequences so disastrous, still the soundness of any construction which would bring one organ of the government into collision with another, is to be more than suspected; for where collision occurs, it is evident the machine is working in a way the framers of it did not intend. But what I want more immediately to press on the attention, is, the necessity of yielding to the acts of the legislature the same respect that is claimed for the acts of the judiciary. Repugnance to the constitution is not always self evident; for questions involving the consideration of its existence, require for their solution the most vigorous exertion of the higher faculties of the mind, and conflicts will be inevitable, if any branch is to apply the constitution after its own fashion to the acts of all the others. I take it, then, the legislature is entitled to all the deference that is due to the judiciary; that its acts are in no case to be treated as *ipso facto* void, except where they would produce a revolution in the government; and that, to avoid them, requires the act of some tribunal competent under the constitution, (if any such there be,) to pass on their validity. All that remains, therefore, is to inquire whether the judiciary or the people are that tribunal.

Now, as the judiciary is not expressly constituted for that purpose, it must derive whatever authority of the sort it may possess, from the reasonableness and fitness of the thing. But, in theory, all the organs of the government are of equal capacity; or, if not equal, each must be supposed to have superior capacity only for those things which peculiarly belong to it; and, as legislation peculiarly involves the consideration of those limitations which are put on the law-making power, and the interpretation of the laws when made, involves only the construction of the laws themselves, it follows that the construction of the constitution in this particular belongs to the legislature, which ought therefore to be taken to have superior capacity to judge of the constitutionality of its own acts. But suppose all to be of equal capacity in every respect, why should one exercise a controlling power over the rest? That the judiciary is of superior rank, has never been pretended, although it has been said to be co-ordinate. It is not easy, however, to comprehend how the power which gives law to all the rest, can be of no more than equal rank with one which receives it, and is answerable to the former for the observance of its statutes. . . .

The power is said to be restricted to cases that are free from doubt or difficulty. But the abstract existence of a power cannot depend on the clearness or obscurity of the case in which it is to be exercised; for that is a consideration that cannot present itself, before the question of the existence of the power shall have been determined; and, if its existence be conceded, no considerations of policy arising from the obscurity of the particular case, ought to influence the exercise of it. . . .

But the judges are sworn to support the constitution, and are they not bound by it as the law of the land? In some respects they are. In the very few cases in which the judiciary, and not the legislature, is the immediate organ to execute its provisions, they are bound by it in preference to any act of assembly to the contrary. In such cases, the constitution is a rule to the courts. But what I have in view in this inquiry, is the supposed right of the judiciary, to interfere, in cases where the constitution is to be carried into effect through the instrumentality of the legislature, and where that organ must necessarily first decide on the constitutionality of its own act. The oath to support the constitution is not peculiar to the judges, but is taken indiscriminately by every officer of the government, and is designed rather as a test of the political principles of the man, than to bind the officer in the discharge of his duty: otherwise it were difficult to determine what operation it is to have in the case of a recorder of deeds, for instance, who, in the execution of his office, has nothing to do with the constitution. But granting it to relate to the official conduct of the judge, as well as every other officer, and not to his political principles, still it must be understood in reference to supporting the constitution, *only as far as that may be involved in his official duty;* and, consequently, if his official duty does not comprehend an inquiry into the authority of the legislature, neither does his oath. . . .

But do not the judges do a *positive act* in violation of the constitution, when they give effect to an unconstitutional law? Not if the law has been passed according to the forms established in the constitution. The fallacy of the question is, in supposing that the judiciary adopts the acts of the legislature as its own; whereas the enactment of a law and the interpretation of it are not concurrent acts, and as the judiciary is not required to concur in the enactment, neither is it in the breach of the constitution which may be the consequence of the enactment. The fault is imputable to the legislature, and on it the responsibility exclusively rests. In this respect, the judges are in the predicament of jurors who are bound to serve in capital cases, although unable, under any circumstances, to reconcile it to their duty to deprive a human being of life. To one of these, who applied to be discharged from the panel, I once heard it remarked, by an eminent and humane judge, "*You* do not deprive a prisoner of life by finding him guilty of a capital crime: you but pronounce his case to be within the law, and it is therefore those who declare the law, and not you, who deprive him of life."

That every thing addressed to the legislature by way of positive command, is purely directory, will hardly be disputed: it is only to enforce prohibitions that the interposition of judicial authority is thought to be warrantable. But I can see no room for a distinction between the injunctions that are positive and those that are negative: the same authority must enforce both.

But it has been said, that this construction would deprive the citizen of advantages which are peculiar to a written constitution, by at once declaring the power of the legislature, in practice, to be illimitable. I ask, what are those advantages? . . . In the business of government, a recurrence to first principles answers the end of an observation at sea with a view to correct the dead reckoning; and, for this purpose, a written constitution is an instrument of inestimable value. It is of inestimable value, also, in rendering its principles familiar to the mass of the people; for, after all, there is no effectual guard against legislative usurpation but public opinion, the force of which, in this country, is inconceivably great. Happily this is proved, by experience, to be a sufficient guard against palpable infractions. The constitution of this state has withstood the shocks of strong party excitement for thirty years, during which no act of the legislature has been declared unconstitutional, although the judiciary has constantly asserted a right to do so in clear cases. But it would be absurd to say, that this remarkable observance of the constitution has been produced, not by the responsibility of the legislature to the people, but by an apprehension of control by the judiciary. Once let public opinion be so corrupt as to sanction every misconstruction of the constitution and abuse of power which the temptation of the moment may dictate, and the party which may happen to be predominant, will laugh at the puny efforts of a dependent power to arrest it in its course.

For these reasons, I am of opinion that it rests with the people, in whom full and absolute sovereign power resides to correct abuses in legislation, by instructing their representatives to repeal the obnoxious act. What is wanting to plenary power in

the government, is reserved by the people for their own immediate use; and to redress an infringement of their rights in this
respect, would seem to be an accessory of the power thus reserved. It might, perhaps, have been better to vest the power in
the judiciary; as it might be expected that its habits of deliberation, and the aid derived from the arguments of counsel, would
more frequently lead to accurate conclusions. On the other
hand, the judiciary is not infallible; and an error by it would admit of no remedy but a more distinct expression of the public
will, through the extraordinary medium of a convention;
whereas, an error by the legislature admits of a remedy by an exertion of the same will, in the ordinary exercise of the right of
suffrage,—a mode better calculated to attain the end, without
popular excitement. It may be said, the people would probably
not notice an error of their representatives. But they would as
probably do so, as notice an error of the judiciary; and, beside,
it is a *postulate* in the theory of our government, and the very
basis of the superstructure, that the people are wise, virtuous,
and competent to manage their own affairs. . . .

⚜   ⚜   ⚜

If Justice Gibson's approach to constitutional review had prevailed in 1803, John Marshall could not have struck down the
statute giving the Supreme Court the power to issue the writ
Marbury sought. That would not have affected Marshall's ability to chastise Thomas Jefferson, though. All he needed to do
was interpret the *statute* as denying the Court that power. And,
indeed, most modern commentators think that Marshall
stretched the statute so that he could establish the Court's
power to strike statutes down.

In the short run, then, deciding that the Court did not have

the power to invalidate statutes would not have affected either
the outcome of Marbury's case or the political disparagement of
Thomas Jefferson that Marshall apparently wanted to convey.
Even in the longer run, such a decision might not have had
much effect. The Supreme Court did not explicitly strike down
any national laws between 1803 and 1857 (see Chapter 3). Instead, it issued opinions saying that congressional statutes had
to be interpreted in ways that made them constitutional rather
than unconstitutional. The Court's power to invalidate national statutes remained relatively unimportant until the twentieth century. (Indeed, the Supreme Court did not strike down
a national statute for violating the Constitution's protection of
freedom of speech until 1968.) It was of course much more vigorous in striking down *state* statutes, but notice that Justice
Gibson's "dissent" relies heavily on the proposition that the
courts and the legislature are coordinate—that is, equal—
branches of the government. That is not true when the Court
deals with state legislation, because the Constitution's supremacy clause makes it clear that national institutions such as
Congress and the federal courts are "above" state legislatures
with respect to the national Constitution.

Justice Gibson made several arguments against judicial review. First, people assumed that legislatures had to comply with
court decisions finding their statutes unconstitutional. But,
Justice Gibson asked, why was that so? Only because legislatures should respect the decisions of their coequal branches.
Justice Gibson then wondered why that argument did not work
just as well the other way. Why shouldn't the courts have to respect the decisions made by legislatures?

Second, judicial review placed the courts and legislatures in
direct conflict. Justice Gibson feared that legislatures might win
any battles with the courts, which, as Alexander Hamilton had

observed while the Constitution was being debated, had neither the sword nor the purse—that is, neither physical nor
financial force—to use against recalcitrant legislators. Legislatures, Justice Gibson observed, had "the strong arm of power."
But, Justice Gibson worried about what would happen even if
the courts won their battles, because any constitution that created the possibilities of this kind of conflict was flawed.

But how could constitutional restrictions be honored without some device like judicial review? Justice Gibson relied on a
theory today known as *popular constitutionalism,* as mentioned
in the Introduction. The people would be vigilant in defense of
the constitution they created and that protected them. Legislation that violated constitutional rights would become the subject of political controversy, and if the people concluded that
the statute did indeed violate the Constitution, they would tell
their legislators to repeal the statute, or would replace those legislators with others who, in the view of the people, would
honor the Constitution.

Many today are skeptical about popular constitutionalism.
The people, they fear, might be caught up in the passions of the
moment and might support rather than oppose unconstitutional legislation. Defenders of popular constitutionalism have
several responses. They suggest that the people have become
inattentive to the Constitution precisely because the courts
have used the power of judicial review so vigorously. Why
bother to worry about the Constitution if the courts will bail us
out anyway? And, after all, as Justice Gibson observed, the
courts are not infallible, either. They can be caught up in
the passions of the moment, too—and they have been, as we'll
see in Chapter 9. Even more, and again as Justice Gibson observed, the Constitution's meaning is rarely transparent. What
one person thinks is an obvious constitutional violation, an-

other thinks is a reasonable exercise of national power. Where these disagreements are reasonable ones, why should they be resolved by judicial declaration rather than through ordinary political discussions? Again, we have to keep judicial fallibility in mind: of course fallible legislatures might enact unconstitutional statutes, but fallible courts with the power of judicial review might strike down ones that are perfectly constitutional.

Justice Gibson's "dissent" would be troubling, though, when a national majority took advantage of its political power to gain advantages at the expense of minorities, or to stifle dissent from advocates of widely despised positions. These are circumstances when "the people" would *want* to violate the Constitution—to adopt statutes that went against any reasonable understanding of the Constitution. Defenders of popular constitutionalism stress how rare these circumstances have been in U.S. history. Most—though not all—of the examples people offer of plainly unconstitutional statutes come from state and local legislatures, and Justice Gibson's "dissent" would allow the national courts to strike down such statutes. Defending the Constitution's design, James Madison pointed out how hard it was to get national legislation enacted—an observation that recent experiences with congressional "gridlock" may have confirmed. And, of course, nothing can guarantee that courts will invalidate all—and only—the unconstitutional statutes Congress does enact.

Defenders of popular constitutionalism have an optimistic view of the people's attachment to the Constitution. They believe that we have an attractive image of what it means to be an American, devoted to the Constitution. Their optimism may be misplaced, but they stress judicial fallibility and, even more, the possibility that the people have been "miseducated" by the twentieth-century experience with a system in which judicial review has played such a large role. Had Justice Gibson's "dissent" prevailed, perhaps a vigilant populace would have kept Congress from enacting the statutes that the courts did strike down. If so, the world of popular constitutionalism might not look that different from the one we inhabit today—except that it would have been created by a people attentive to the Constitution rather than by courts.

CHAPTER 2

"Experience should teach us wisdom."

McCulloch v. Maryland, 1819

James Madison remembered the Constitutional Convention of 1787. After all, he had been one of the convention's most important figures, and he kept reasonably detailed notes of what people said. One of the key issues during the convention was how powerful the national government would be. The so called anti-Federalists, who feared a strong national government, insisted that the new government's powers be "few and defined," as Madison put it in newspaper articles urging New York's voters to support the proposed constitution. Indicating its sensitivity to these concerns, the convention rejected a proposal to give the new Congress the power to charter corporations, and in particular the power to create a national bank.

Once the Constitution was adopted, though, Andrew Hamilton, the first secretary of the treasury, urged in the strongest terms that a national bank was necessary if the national government were to be fiscally stable and responsible. James Madison, representing Virginia in the House of Representatives, made a powerful speech against the constitutionality of Hamilton's proposal. President George Washington asked his cabinet members for their opinions. Secretary of State Thomas Jefferson supported the views of Madison, his fellow Virginian, but Washington ended up agreeing with Hamilton and signed the legislation creating the Bank of the United States.

The statute gave the Bank a twenty-year charter. When that period expired, Congress let the Bank go out of business. Five years later Congress changed its mind. The nation had experienced a period of inflation and, perhaps more important, serious financial disruptions brought about by the War of 1812. Congress created the Second Bank of the United States in 1816. By then James Madison was president. Saying that twenty-five years of experience and the judgments made by the First Federal Congress and the first president settled the matter, Madison withdrew from his prior constitutional objections and signed the law.

The Jeffersonian Democratic Party remained concerned that the national government was too powerful, and the Second Bank of the United States became the poster child for their concerns. Controlling legislatures in several states, the Democrats enacted statutes hostile to the Bank. Maryland's legislature imposed a tax on the Bank's operations. James McCulloch, the manager of the Baltimore branch, refused to pay the tax, arguing that the tax was unconstitutional. The state courts upheld the tax.

John Marshall took the opportunity provided by *McCulloch v. Maryland* to set forth his nationalist constitutional views. The state argued that it could impose whatever tax it wanted on the Bank because Congress did not have any power to create the Bank in the first place. Marshall spent most of his opinion dealing with that claim.

Marshall's problem was that nothing in the Constitution specifically gave Congress the power to charter a corporation or create a Bank. Indeed, Maryland's lawyers argued, the Tenth Amendment should be read to *bar* Congress from doing so. The Tenth Amendment grew out of a provision in the Articles of Confederation, the document that created the nation's government from U.S. independence in 1776 to 1789, stating that the states retained "every power, jurisdiction, and right, which is not by this Confederation expressly delegated to the United States." Marshall pointed out that the Tenth Amendment was different, because it omitted the word "expressly": "The powers not delegated to the United States by the Constitution, nor prohibited by it to the States, are reserved to the States respectively, or to the people."

Still, that was not enough to get Marshall where he needed to go. What he needed was something in the Constitution that *gave* Congress the power to create a bank. He found it at the end of the Constitution's list of congressional powers: "The Congress shall have power ... To make all laws which shall be necessary and proper for carrying into execution the foregoing powers." The state's lawyers said that these were *restrictive* rather than expansive terms. Something had to be really or strictly necessary to implement one of the listed powers. Marshall responded that the term "necessary" meant something like "convenient" or "desirable," rather than "absolutely necessary," a term that he pointed out was used elsewhere in the Constitution.

Even that was not enough to solve Marshall's problem. Maybe a national bank was convenient or useful—but it had to be useful to accomplishing something listed elsewhere in the Constitution. And here Marshall turned to nationalist imagery: "Throughout this vast republic, from the St. Croix to the Gulf of Mexico, from the Atlantic to the Pacific, revenue is to be collected and expended, armies are to be marched and supported. The exigencies of the nation may require, that the treasure raised in the north should be transported to the south, that raised in the east, conveyed to the west, or that this order should be reversed. Is that construction of the constitution to be preferred, which would render these operations difficult, hazardous and expensive?" Having a national bank whose notes would be accepted throughout the country would make it much easier—convenient—to carry out these national goals.

Like *Marbury, McCulloch* was a unanimous opinion. The Second Bank of the United States operated for a decade but remained controversial in politics. Andrew Jackson, whose presidential bid in 1824 failed because of what his supporters called a "corrupt bargain" between his adversaries, was elected in 1828 on a platform that included opposition to the Second Bank as another example of corruption. Thinking that they could weaken Jackson politically, his opponents brought forward a bill to reauthorize the Bank in 1832, several years before they had to but in the middle of an election year. Jackson's veto of the bill they produced, delivered on July 10, 1832, amounts to a "dissent" from *McCulloch*.

⚜   ⚜   ⚜

To the Senate.

The bill "to modify and continue" the act entitled "An act to incorporate the subscribers to the Bank of the United States" was presented to me on the 4th July instant. Having considered it with that solemn regard to the principles of the Constitution which the day was calculated to inspire, and come to the conclusion that it ought not to become a law, I herewith return it to the Senate, in which it originated, with my objections.

A bank of the United States is in many respects convenient for the Government and useful to the people. Entertaining this opinion, and deeply impressed with the belief that some of the powers and privileges possessed by the existing bank are unauthorized by the Constitution, subversive of the rights of the States, and dangerous to the liberties of the people, I felt it my duty at an early period of my Administration to call the attention of Congress to the practicability of organizing an institution combining all its advantages and obviating these objections. I sincerely regret that in the act before me I can perceive none of those modifications of the bank charter which are necessary, in my opinion, to make it compatible with justice, with sound policy, or with the Constitution of our country.

If the opinion of the Supreme Court covered the whole ground of this act, it ought not to control the coordinate authorities of this Government. The Congress, the Executive, and the Court must each for itself be guided by its own opinion of the Constitution. Each public officer who takes an oath to support the Constitution swears that he will support it as he understands it, and not as it is understood by others. It is as much the duty of the House of Representatives, of the Senate, and of the President to decide upon the constitutionality of any bill or resolution which may be presented to them for passage or approval as it is of the supreme judges when it may be brought before them for judicial decision. The opinion of the judges has no more authority over Congress than the opinion of Congress has over the judges, and on that point the President is independent of both. The authority of the Supreme Court must not, therefore, be permitted to control the Congress or the Executive when acting in their legislative capacities, but to have only such influence as the force of their reasoning may deserve....

... Under the decision of the Supreme Court, therefore, it is the exclusive province of Congress and the President to decide whether the particular features of this act are *necessary* and *proper* in order to enable the bank to perform conveniently and efficiently the public duties assigned to it as a fiscal agent, and therefore constitutional, or *unnecessary* and *improper,* and therefore unconstitutional....

... [L]et us examine the details of this act in accordance

with the rule of legislative action which they have laid down. It will be found that many of the powers and privileges conferred on it can not be supposed necessary for the purpose for which it is proposed to be created, and are not, therefore, means necessary to attain the end in view, and consequently not justified by the Constitution.

On two subjects only does the Constitution recognize in Congress the power to grant exclusive privileges or monopolies. It declares that "Congress shall have power to promote the progress of science and useful arts by securing for limited times to authors and inventors the exclusive right to their respective writings and discoveries." Out of this express delegation of power have grown our laws of patents and copyrights. As the Constitution expressly delegates to Congress the power to grant exclusive privileges in these cases as the means of executing the substantive power "to promote the progress of science and useful arts," it is consistent with the fair rules of construction to conclude that such a power was not intended to be granted as a means of accomplishing any other end. On every other subject which comes within the scope of Congressional power there is an ever-living discretion in the use of proper means, which can not be restricted or abolished without an amendment of the Constitution. Every act of Congress, therefore, which attempts by grants of monopolies or sale of exclusive privileges for a limited time, or a time without limit, to restrict or extinguish its own discretion in the choice of means to execute its delegated powers is equivalent to a legislative amendment of the Constitution, and palpably unconstitutional. . . .

The several States reserved the power at the formation of the Constitution to regulate and control titles and transfers of real property, and most, if not all, of them have laws disqualifying aliens from acquiring or holding lands within their limits. But this act, in disregard of the undoubted right of the States to prescribe such disqualifications, gives to aliens stockholders in this bank an interest and title, as members of the corporation, to all the real property it may acquire within any of the States of this Union. This privilege granted to aliens is not *"necessary"* to enable the bank to perform its public duties, nor in any sense *"proper,"* because it is vitally subversive of the rights of the States. . . .

By its silence, considered in connection with the decision of the Supreme Court in the case of McCulloch against the State of Maryland, this act takes from the States the power to tax a portion of the banking business carried on within their limits, in subversion of one of the strongest barriers which secured them against Federal encroachments. Banking, like farming, manufacturing, or any other occupation or profession, is a *business,* the right to follow which is not originally derived from the laws. Every citizen and every company of citizens in all of our States possessed the right until the State legislatures deemed it good policy to prohibit private banking by law. If the prohibitory State laws were now repealed, every citizen would again possess the right. The State banks are a qualified restoration of the right which has been taken away by the laws against banking, guarded by such provisions and limitations as in the opinion of the State legislatures the public interest requires. These corporations, unless there be an exemption in their charter, are, like private bankers and banking companies, subject to State taxation. The manner in which these taxes shall be laid depends wholly on legislative discretion. It may be upon the bank, upon the stock, upon the profits, or in any other mode which the sovereign power shall will.

Upon the formation of the Constitution the States guarded their taxing power with peculiar jealousy. They surrendered it only as it regards imports and exports. In relation to every other object within their jurisdiction, whether persons, property, business, or professions, it was secured in as ample a manner as it was before possessed. All persons, though United States officers, are liable to a poll tax by the States within which they reside. The lands of the United States are liable to the usual land tax, except in the new States, from whom agreements that they will not tax unsold lands are exacted when they are admitted into the Union. Horses, wagons, any beasts or vehicles, tools, or property belonging to private citizens, though employed in the service of the United States, are subject to State taxation. Every private business, whether carried on by an officer of the General Government or not, whether it be mixed with public concerns or not, even if it be carried on by the Government of the United States itself, separately or in partnership, falls within the scope of the taxing power of the State. Nothing comes more fully within it than banks and the business of banking, by whomsoever instituted and carried on. Over this whole subject-matter it is just as absolute, unlimited, and uncontrollable as if the Constitution had never been adopted, because in the formation of that instrument it was reserved without qualification. . . .

It can not be *necessary* to the character of the bank as a fiscal agent of the Government that its private business should be exempted from that taxation to which all the State banks are liable, nor can I conceive it "*proper*" that the substantive and most essential powers reserved by the States shall be thus attacked and annihilated as a means of executing the powers delegated to the General Government. It may be safely assumed that none of those sages who had an agency in forming or adopting our Constitution ever imagined that any portion of the taxing power of the States not prohibited to them nor delegated to Congress was to be swept away and annihilated as a means of executing certain powers delegated to Congress. . . .

Experience should teach us wisdom. Most of the difficulties our Government now encounters and most of the dangers

which impend over our Union have sprung from an abandon-
ment of the legitimate objects of Government by our national
legislation, and the adoption of such principles as are embodied
in this act. Many of our rich men have not been content with
equal protection and equal benefits, but have besought us to
make them richer by act of Congress. By attempting to gratify
their desires we have in the results of our legislation arrayed section against section, interest against interest, and man against
man, in a fearful commotion which threatens to shake the
foundations of our Union. It is time to pause in our career to review our principles, and if possible revive that devoted patriot-
ism and spirit of compromise which distinguished the sages of
the Revolution and the fathers of our Union. If we can not at
once, in justice to interests vested under improvident legislation, make our Government what it ought to be, we can at least
take a stand against all new grants of monopolies and exclusive
privileges, against any prostitution of our Government to the
advancement of the few at the expense of the many, and in favor of compromise and gradual reform in our code of laws and
system of political economy.

I have now done my duty to my country. If sustained by my
fellow citizens, I shall be grateful and happy; if not, I shall find
in the motives which impel me ample grounds for contentment
and peace. In the difficulties which surround us and the dangers which threaten our institutions there is cause for neither
dismay nor alarm. For relief and deliverance let us firmly rely
on that kind Providence which I am sure watches with peculiar
care over the destinies of our Republic, and on the intelligence
and wisdom of our countrymen. Through His abundant good-
ness and their patriotic devotion our liberty and Union will be
preserved.

The Second Bank of the United States had been operating for a decade and a half when Jackson vetoed its recharter. Suppose the Court had agreed with him in 1819 and stopped the Bank then. The national financial system would have developed in a somewhat different form, but it would have developed anyway. Banks chartered by the states would have sprung up, and they would have entered into contracts under which a bank in one state would accept notes issued by a contractual partner in another state. The system might have been a bit more costly to operate than the Second Bank of the United States was, but competition among state-level banks might have reduced the mismanagement and corruption that came to characterize the Second Bank of the United States. The economic consequences of Jackson's constitutional position in 1819 would probably have been small.

Jackson's "dissent" from *McCulloch* contains two themes. First, he asserts that as president he has a constitutional right, indeed a duty, to assess the constitutionality of proposed legislation *on his own*. He is not, he says, bound by the Supreme Court's prior determination in *McCulloch* that the Constitution gives Congress the power to create the Bank. Second, he disagrees with the Court's interpretation of the scope of national power in *McCulloch*.

In some contexts, the view Jackson asserts of his independent power to determine whether a proposed statute is unconstitutional is entirely uncontroversial. That view, sometimes called *departmentalism*, holds that a legislator can oppose a statute on constitutional grounds even after the Supreme Court has held it to be constitutional, that the president can veto legislation he believes to be unconstitutional as Jackson did, and that the president can pardon people convicted of violating national laws the president believes to be unconstitutional even after the courts have upheld their convictions (as Thomas Jefferson did).

Departmentalism is more controversial in other settings. Suppose one president signs a statute that his successor believes to be unconstitutional. Can the president simply refuse to enforce the statute—even if Congress remains convinced that the statute is constitutional? That is a formula for serious tension between the president and Congress. Most presidents have asserted the departmentalist position in this setting, but have been cautious about how aggressively to pursue it. Typically, they defend their position until a court rules against them, and then accede to the court's decision. The most famous recent example comes from the end of Richard Nixon's presidency. After tape recordings of incriminating conversations in the Oval Office were discovered, Nixon made two claims: first, that the conversations were covered by executive privilege, and second, the departmentalist claim that only he could decide whether the claim of executive privilege was constitutionally valid. Yet, when the Supreme Court ruled that his assertion of executive privilege had to give way to a grand jury demand for the material, Nixon turned the material over and resigned. Not all of these problems get into court, though, and some are "resolved" politically: Congress gives in, or subjects the president to subpoenas, oversight hearings, restrictions on funding, and the like, until the political costs to the president exceed the benefits he gains from refusing to enforce the law.

Even more controversial are cases where the courts find a statute *unconstitutional* and the president disagrees. Here, too, the most aggressive presidents have *asserted* the departmentalist position, claiming that they have the power to continue to apply a statute the courts have found unconstitutional. In a constitutional world where *Marbury* and the courts' power of judicial review is deeply embedded in the constitutional culture, this really *is* a formula for constitutional crisis, and presidents have never pushed their departmentalist views to the point of crisis. Couple departmentalism with popular constitutionalism (Chapter 1), though, and we might have quite a different constitutional world and culture. Note that Jackson's concluding paragraph alludes to popular constitutionalism through its implicit reference to the forthcoming election of 1832.

Jackson's second theme was about what the Constitution meant. *McCulloch* was wrong, Jackson said, to interpret the "necessary and proper" clause as broadly as it did. Such an interpretation, Jackson argued, left the national government open to corruption by "rich men" who get unjustifiable monopolies from the national government that they could not get from state governments. The defense against such corruption was to narrow the national government's powers. Jackson's veto message does not make it clear precisely *what* the limit on the powers should be. He suggests that exercises of national power that interfere with important powers state governments have might be unconstitutional, but the specific grounds for his "dissent" from *McCulloch* are more limited—to the direct interference the Bank creates with the states' power to tax, and with the interference with state regulations of ownership of property by noncitizens. And his objection to the Bank's "monopoly" preserves a rather wide "ever-living discretion" in Congress.

The Jacksonian view of the Constitution prevailed for several decades. The Bank's charter expired in 1836 and the nation went without a central bank until the early twentieth century. (Some economic historians attribute the depression of 1837 to the Bank's demise, though others disagree.) Not until 1887 did Congress begin to exercise wide power to regulate aspects of the national economy. And only in the twentieth century did the national government become the large regulatory institution we are now familiar with. In a sense, then, Jackson's "dissent" was constitutional law for much of the nineteenth century.

What are its implications for today's national government? Because the legal position asserted in the veto message is not entirely clear, perhaps its implications are few. Certainly good lawyers could defend a great deal of the national regulatory system as within Congress's "ever-living discretion." National environmental laws deal with the effects that pollution in one state has on other states, and on nearly every sensible interpretation of national power the national government would have the power to regulate activities in one state that have effects in others. At the same time, Jackson's attention to the states' own regulatory powers would caution against expansive claims on Congress's behalf. A Jacksonian might raise questions about national regulation of workplace safety, for example. A contemporary "Jacksonian" government might look a lot like the one we have, but it might instead leave much of what the national government does today to the states.

CHAPTER 3

"Among those for whom and whose posterity the Constitution was ordained and established."

Dred Scott v. Sanford, 1857

Slavery was the contradiction at the Constitution's heart. Criticizing the American drive to revolution, Samuel Johnson asked, "How is it that we hear the loudest yelps for liberty among the drivers of Negroes?" The Constitution's framers were sufficiently embarrassed by slavery that they omitted the word and its variants from the Constitution, but they could not avoid the issue. Several constitutional provisions clearly referred to slavery without using the term, and—more important—the Constitution's structure was designed to assure the South that it would have enough political power to protect slavery against national regulation.

That structure worked well enough for a while. Agitation in the North against slavery annoyed Southerners, and Thomas Jefferson thought that the explicit intrusion of slavery into politics was like "a fire bell in the night," filling him "with terror." Jefferson was referring to the Missouri Compromise of 1820, in which Northerners agreed to allow slavery in newly acquired territories—and new states—in Missouri and below, and Southerners agreed to a prohibition on slavery northward. Managing the slavery issue through politics became increasingly awkward for the South over the next decades. South Carolina's John C. Calhoun developed a novel constitutional theory, which would have required Southern agreement to any policy affecting the South even in the face of majority support in the nation as a whole.

By the 1850s the prospects for permanently managing the conflict over slavery through politics seemed quite dim. Dred Scott's suit for freedom seemed to provide a possible solution— resolve the conflict through a definitive judicial ruling. Indeed, knowing from leaks he got through his friends on the Supreme Court that the case was about to be decided in a way favorable to the South, President James Buchanan made a public statement urging people to wait for, and then accept, the Court's decision.

Dred Scott was the slave of Dr. John Emerson, an army surgeon who served for several years in Illinois, a free state, and Minnesota, a free territory under the Missouri Compromise. After further travels with Emerson and his family, Scott and his wife Harriet ended up in Missouri, a slave state. In 1846 the Scotts filed a "freedom suit" in the Missouri state courts, claiming that their residence in Illinois and Minnesota had conferred freedom on them. That claim had some support in Missouri law, but with the issue of slavery increasingly troublesome nationally, the Missouri courts changed course and in 1852, after a series of delays in the lawsuit, held that the Scotts' "voluntary" return to Missouri meant that they were still slaves.

By the time the Missouri courts ruled, Dr. Emerson had died, his widow had remarried, and she had given her brother John Sandford authority over her slaves. (Sandford's name was misspelled in the Supreme Court's decision.) These developments opened a new path for the litigation. Sandford was a resident of New York, and Scott's lawyers decided to file a new freedom suit in *federal* court. They invoked a constitutional provision (referred to as the "diversity" jurisdiction) saying that a citizen of one state could use the federal courts to sue a citizen of another state.

Sandford's lawyers responded with a barrage of defenses. As a slave or former slave, they argued, Scott could not be a citizen of the United States and therefore could not use the diversity jurisdiction. Nor could he have been freed by his residence in Minnesota, because Congress did not have the power to prohibit slavery in the territories: the Missouri Compromise was unconstitutional. And, even if Congress had the power to enact the Missouri Compromise, Congress could not insist that slaves taken into the "free" territories were indeed free because doing so would deprive their owners of property without "due process of law."

The Supreme Court accepted *all* of these defenses. Initially a majority of the Court hoped to issue a relatively narrow ruling on an arcane technical point. Justice James Wayne, a Georgian, pushed the majority to its broader rulings. The majority held that Congress did not have the power to prohibit slavery in the territories, that doing so deprived slaveowners who moved to the territories of their property without due process of law, and that Americans of African origin whose ancestors had been held as slaves could not be citizens of the United States. Justice Benjamin Curtis of Massachusetts then decided to dissent.

Mr. Justice Curtis, dissenting. . . .

[U]nder the allegations contained in this plea, and admitted by the demurrer, the question is, whether any person of African descent, whose ancestors were sold as slaves in the United

States, can be a citizen of the United States. If any such person can be a citizen, this plaintiff has the right to the judgment of the court that he is so; for no cause is shown by the plea why he is not so, except his descent and the slavery of his ancestors.

The first section of the second article of the Constitution uses the language, 'a citizen of the United States at the time of the adoption of the Constitution.' One mode of approaching this question is, to inquire who were citizens of the United States at the time of the adoption of the Constitution. . . .

To determine whether any free persons, descended from Africans held in slavery, were citizens of the United States under the Confederation, and consequently at the time of the adoption of the Constitution of the United States, it is only necessary to know whether any such persons were citizens of either of the States under the Confederation, at the time of the adoption of the Constitution.

Of this there can be no doubt. At the time of the ratification of the Articles of Confederation, all free native-born inhabitants of the States of New Hampshire, Massachusetts, New York, New Jersey, and North Carolina, though descended from African slaves, were not only citizens of those States, but such of them as had the other necessary qualifications possessed the franchise of electors, on equal terms with other citizens. . . .

The first section of the second article of the Constitution uses the language, 'a natural-born citizen.' It thus assumes that citizenship may be acquired by birth. Undoubtedly, this language of the Constitution was used in reference to that principle of public law, well understood in this country at the time of the adoption of the Constitution, which referred citizenship to the place of birth. At the Declaration of Independence, and ever since, the received general doctrine has been, in conformity with the common law, that free persons born within either of the colonies were subjects of the King; that by the Declaration of Independence, and the consequent acquisition of sovereignty by the several States, all such persons ceased to be subjects, and became citizens of the several States, except so far as some of them were disfranchised by the legislative power of the States. . . .

Laying aside, then, the case of aliens, concerning which the Constitution of the United States has provided, and confining our view to free persons born within the several States, we find that the Constitution has recognised the general principle of public law, that allegiance and citizenship depend on the place of birth; that it has not attempted practically to apply this principle by designating the particular classes of persons who should or should not come under it; that when we turn to the Constitution for an answer to the question, what free persons, born within the several States, are citizens of the United States, the only answer we can receive from any of its express provisions is, the citizens of the several States are to enjoy the privileges and immunities of citizens in every State, and their franchise as electors under the Constitution depends on their citizenship in the several States. Add to this, that the Constitution was ordained by the citizens of the several States; that they were 'the people of the United States,' for whom and whose posterity the Government was declared in the preamble of the Constitution to be made; that each of them was 'a citizen of the United States at the time of the adoption of the Constitution,' within the meaning of those words in that instrument; that by them the Government was to be and was in fact organized; and that no power is conferred on the Government of the Union to discriminate between them, or to disfranchise any of them— the necessary conclusion is, that those persons born within the several States, who, by force of their respective Constitutions and laws, are citizens of the State, are thereby citizens of the United States.

It may be proper here to notice some supposed objections to this view of the subject.

It has been often asserted that the Constitution was made exclusively by and for the white race. It has already been shown that in five of the thirteen original States, colored persons then possessed the elective franchise, and were among those by whom the Constitution was ordained and established. If so, it is not true, in point of fact, that the Constitution was made exclusively by the white race. And that it was made exclusively for the white race is, in my opinion, not only an assumption not warranted by anything in the Constitution, but contradicted by its opening declaration, that it was ordained and established by the people of the United States, for themselves and their posterity. And as free colored persons were then citizens of at least five States, and so in every sense part of the people of the United States, they were among those for whom and whose posterity the Constitution was ordained and established. . . .

It has been further objected, that if free colored persons, born within a particular State, and made citizens of that State by its Constitution and laws, are thereby made citizens of the United States, then, under the second section of the fourth article of the Constitution, such persons would be entitled to all the privileges and immunities of citizens in the several States; and if so, then colored persons could vote, and be eligible to not only Federal offices, but offices even in those States whose Constitution and laws disqualify colored persons from voting or being elected to office.

But this position rests upon an assumption which I deem untenable. Its basis is, that no one can be deemed a citizen of the United States who is not entitled to enjoy all the privileges and franchises which are conferred on any citizen. That this is not true, under the Constitution of the United States, seems to me clear.

... The truth is, that citizenship, under the Constitution of the United States, is not dependent on the possession of any particular political or even of all civil rights; and any attempt so to define it must lead to error. To what citizens the elective franchise shall be confided, is a question to be determined by each State, in accordance with its own views of the necessities or expediencies of its condition. What civil rights shall be enjoyed by its citizens, and whether all shall enjoy the same, or how they may be gained or lost, are to be determined in the same way.

One may confine the right of suffrage to white male citizens; another may extend it to colored persons and females; one may allow all persons above a prescribed age to convey property and transact business; another may exclude married women. But whether native-born women, or persons under age, or under guardianship because insane or spendthrifts, be excluded from voting or holding office, or allowed to do so, I apprehend no one will deny that they are citizens of the United States. Besides, this clause of the Constitution does not confer on the citizens of one State, in all other States, specific and enumerated privileges and immunities. They are entitled to such as belong to citizenship, but not to such as belong to particular citizens attended by other qualifications. Privileges and immunities which belong to certain citizens of a State, by reason of the operation of causes other than mere citizenship, are not conferred. Thus, if the laws of a State require, in addition to citizenship of the State, some qualification for office, or the exercise of the elective franchise, citizens of all other States, coming thither to reside, and not possessing those qualifications, cannot enjoy those privileges, not because they are not to be deemed entitled to the privileges of citizens of the State in which they reside, but because they, in common with the native-born citizens of that State, must have the qualifications prescribed by law for the enjoyment of such privileges, under its Constitution and laws. It rests with the States themselves so to frame their Constitutions and laws as not to attach a particular privilege or immunity to mere naked citizenship. If one of the States will not deny to any of its own citizens a particular privilege or immunity, if it confer it on all of them by reason of mere naked citizenship, then it may be claimed by every citizen of each State by force of the Constitution; and it must be borne in mind, that the difficulties which attend the allowance of the claims of colored persons to be citizens of the United States are not avoided by saying that, though each State may make them its citizens, they are not thereby made citizens of the United States, because the privileges of general citizenship are secured to the citizens of each State. The language of the Constitution is, 'The citizens of each State shall be entitled to all privileges and immunities of citizens in the several States.' If each State may make such persons its citizens, they became, as such, entitled to the benefits of this article, if there be a native-born citizenship of the United States distinct from a native-born citizenship of the several States. . . .

. . . That under this fourth article of the Confederation, free persons of color might be entitled to the privileges of general citizenship, if otherwise entitled thereto, is clear. When this article was, in substance, placed in and made part of the Constitution of the United States, with no change in its language calculated to exclude free colored persons from the benefit of its provisions, the presumption is, to say the least, strong, that the practical effect which it was designed to have, and did have, under the former Government, it was designed to have, and should have, under the new Government. . . .

. . . I will now proceed to examine the question, whether this [due process] clause is entitled to the effect thus attributed to it. It is necessary, first, to have a clear view of the nature and incidents of that particular species of property which is now in question.

Slavery, being contrary to natural right, is created only by municipal law. This is not only plain in itself, and agreed by all writers on the subject, but is inferable from the Constitution, and has been explicitly declared by this court. . . .

Nor, in my judgment, will the position, that a prohibition to bring slaves into a Territory deprives any one of his property without due process of law, bear examination.

It must be remembered that this restriction on the legislative power is not peculiar to the Constitution of the United States; it was borrowed from Magna Charta; was brought to America by our ancestors, as part of their inherited liberties, and has existed in all the States, usually in the very words of the great charter. It existed in every political community in America in 1787, when the ordinance prohibiting slavery north and west of the Ohio was passed.

And if a prohibition of slavery in a Territory in 1820 violated this principle of Magna Charta, the ordinance of 1787 also violated it; and what power had, I do not say the Congress of the Confederation alone, but the Legislature of Virginia, of the Legislature of any or all the States of the Confederacy, to consent to such a violation? The people of the States had conferred no such power. I think I may at least say, if the Congress did then violate Magna Charta by the ordinance, no one discovered that violation. Besides, if the prohibition upon all persons, citizens as well as others, to bring slaves into a Territory, and a declaration that if brought they shall be free, deprives citizens of their property without due process of law, what shall we say of the legislation of many of the slaveholding States which have enacted the same prohibition? As early as October, 1778, a law was passed in Virginia, that thereafter no slave should be imported into that Commonwealth by sea or by land, and that every slave who should be imported should become free. A citizen of Virginia purchased in Maryland a slave who belonged to another citizen of Virginia, and removed with the slave to Virginia. The slave sued for her freedom, and recovered it. . . . I am not aware that such laws, though they exist in many States, were ever supposed to be in conflict with the principle of Magna Charta incorporated into the State Constitutions. It was certainly understood by the Convention which framed the Constitution, and has been so understood ever since, that, under the power to regulate commerce, Congress could prohibit the importation of slaves; and the exercise of the power was restrained till 1808. A citizen of the United States owns slaves in Cuba, and brings them to the United States, where they are set free by the legislation of Congress. Does this legislation deprive him of his property without due process of law? If so, what becomes of the laws prohibiting the slave trade? If not, how can similar regulation respecting a Territory violate the fifth amendment of the Constitution? . . .

⚜   ⚜   ⚜

Dred Scott himself almost certainly would have remained a slave even if Justice Curtis's dissent had prevailed. Justice Curtis would have held that those brought to America as slaves and their descendants could be American citizens and therefore had the right to sue in the national courts. His discussion of what else that meant, though, indicates that having the right to sue did not imply that such a person had all the rights that *state* citizens had. In particular, Justice Curtis would have left it to the states to decide who was a state citizen. True, Justice Curtis would have held that Congress had the power to ban slavery in the territories, and that interpreting that ban to mean that slaves taken into the territories were freed by that very action did not deprive slaveowners of their property without due process of law—both holdings the Court majority rejected. It would have taken an additional step, which Justice Curtis said nothing about, to hold that Congress's ban on slavery in the territories required states to treat as free persons like Scott, who had been taken to the territories and then returned without immediate objection to a slave state. Justice Curtis implied that Scott's status as slave or free was something for the Missouri courts to decide. And, they had already decided in Scott's own case that his time in Minnesota did not convert him into a permanently free person.

The Civil War effectively ended slavery, which was outlawed by the Thirteenth Amendment (1866), and the precise issue the Dred Scott case raised would of course never arise again. Adopted in 1868, the Fourteenth Amendment's first sentence rejected the majority's holding, stating that every person born within the territory of the United States and subject to its jurisdiction—a phrase designed to exempt children of diplomats and, probably, Native Americans—was a citizen of the United States and of the state in which he resided. The idea of "birthright citizenship" has come under some pressure recently, with some conservative legal theorists arguing that children born in the United States of parents who are in the country illegally should not be entitled to birthright citizenship because, they say, the children should not be understood to be "subject to" the jurisdiction of the United States. This argument is quite strained (no one thinks that the U.S. government cannot prosecute such people for treason, for example), and has not made much headway in the current debates over immigration policy.

Another majority holding has had a longer life. According to the majority, the power the United States government exercises even outside the territorial boundaries of the United States is limited by the Constitution. That was true in the territories, and after the United States acquired sovereignty over Puerto Rico and the Philippines, it was true there as well. The content of particular constitutional rights might vary depending on where the government exercised its power: people in the Philippines might not be entitled to a criminal jury trial, for example, but they could not be subjected to "cruel and unusual punishment" in violation of the Eighth Amendment. This issue has recently been revived in connection with those held as enemy combatants at Guantànamo Bay, Cuba. The Military Commissions Act of 2006 purported to deny such persons a right to have a federal court determine whether the conditions under which they were held violated the Constitution. The majority holding in *Dred Scott* suggests that the detainees should have the right Congress appears to deny them.

Finally, *Dred Scott* is often cited as the first Supreme Court decision enforcing what has come to be called "substantive due process"—the use of the due process clause, whose terms seem to refer only to the procedures government uses, to deny the government the power to regulate property or liberty. Substantive due process flourished in the early twentieth century as a protection for the rights of property owners, then was discredited until the late twentieth century, when it returned as a vehicle for protecting privacy and individual autonomy (see Chapters 6, 13, and 14).

The effects of the Civil War and the Thirteenth and Fourteenth Amendments made the Dred Scott case seem irrelevant for many years, and the decision remains the one Supreme Court decision that only a handful of scholars attempt to defend. In one sense, then, the most interesting question about the decision is this: would the Civil War have occurred—when it did, earlier, later—had Justice Curtis's position prevailed? Putting aside precise questions of timing, the answer is: almost certainly. Chief Justice Taney and President Buchanan hoped that the Court's resolution of the question of whether Congress could prohibit slavery in the territories would damp down sectional tensions. Instead, by effectively holding unconstitutional the central plank of the new Republican Party, the decision energized Northern antislavery politicians. The opinion became central to the debates between Abraham Lincoln and Stephen Douglas that made Lincoln a national figure. But a decision upholding Congress's power to prohibit slavery in the territories would have had the same effect, and perhaps even more. Republicans would have campaigned on a platform of vigorous opposition to slavery's extension, pointing to Justice Curtis's opinion to explain why if elected they had the power to implement their platform. And Southern defenders of slavery would have taken the Court's decision to confirm what they already feared—that slavery was politically vulnerable within the United States, and that preserving slavery might require secession.

The structure of political power in the late 1850s was propelling the nation to war over slavery. Perhaps, as some historians suggested in the 1950s and 1960s, astute statesmanship might have avoided war in the 1860s and perhaps permanently—though at the cost of prolonging slavery. It seems clear, though, that the Dred Scott case had little to do with whether there would be a war to achieve Southern independence or to preserve the Union.

CHAPTER 4

"To enable the black race to take the rank of mere citizens."

The *Civil Rights Cases*, 1883

The end of the Civil War led to a constitutional transformation—or so it might have seemed just after the war. Slavery ended, and Congress was given the power to overcome its legacy by outlawing what people in the 1860s called the "badges and incidents" of slavery. The Fourteenth Amendment created individual rights against *state* governments, by denying the states the power to "abridge the privileges or immunities" of U.S. citizens, or "deprive any person of life, liberty, or property without due process of law," or "deny to any person . . . the equal protection of the laws." The natural reading of these clauses was that they addressed everything a state could do: the "privileges or immunities" clause said that there were some laws that were simply beyond the states' power to enact; the due process clause limited *how* the states were to enforce their laws; and the equal protection clause said that, whatever the states did, they had to do to everybody. Congress got the power to enforce these prohibitions as well.

In the late 1860s Congress took advantage of its new powers. It enacted new civil rights statutes and, probably more important, sent federal troops to occupy the South while governments controlled by freed slaves and their allies tried to reconstruct the Southern social order on a new basis. Within a decade, though, the impulse to remake the South faded, and white Southerners reclaimed their governments. And, perhaps more important, federal troops left the South and Congress gradually drew back from its effort to enforce civil rights.

The end of Reconstruction was signaled by the contested 1876 presidential election, which was resolved by Democrat Rutherford B. Hayes's agreement to withdraw the federal troops from the South. A year earlier, though, Congress had enacted the last major civil rights statute before the revival of the civil rights movement in the 1950s. The Civil Rights Act of 1875 was a public accommodations statute, barring racial discrimination in inns, hotels, theaters, and means of public transportation such as railroads.

The Supreme Court held the 1875 act unconstitutional in the *Civil Rights Cases*. The Court grouped together five cases, involving three different episodes of discrimination at theaters and hotels in New York and San Francisco. The statute's defenders relied on both the Thirteenth and the Fourteenth amendments. Racial discrimination in places of public accommodations was, they said, one of those "badges and incidents" of slavery that Congress could outlaw. The Court's majority responded that racial discrimination was a mere "civil injury," not a legacy of slavery: "When a man has emerged from slavery, and by the aid of beneficent legislation has shaken off the inseparable concomitants of that state, there must be some stage in the progress of his elevation when he takes the rank of a mere citizen, and ceases to be the special favorite of the law...." That time had come by 1883 when the cases reached the Court.

The Fourteenth Amendment, the Court held, addressed only actions by the *states,* which were not involved in the private discriminatory acts of the hotels and restaurants targeted by the statute. The victim of discrimination was of course wronged, but the state had nothing to do with it, and the victim was no less a citizen in the government's eyes. The majority worried that allowing Congress to rely on the Fourteenth Amendment as a basis for the statute would authorize an enormous shift of power from the states to Congress—which, one might have thought, was precisely what the amendment's framers hoped might happen. But the reformist impulse had disappeared, and the Court's approach rapidly became the conventional wisdom.

Justice John Marshall Harlan, himself a former slaveowner, dissented. He began his legal career in Kentucky working for his father. When the Civil War started, Harlan enlisted in the Union Army, then resigned his commission when his father died. He entered politics, running twice and losing twice as the Republican candidate for Kentucky governor. He was appointed to the Supreme Court in 1877 and served until 1911. Oliver Wendell Holmes Jr., who joined Harlan on the Supreme Court in 1902, described Harlan as having a mind like a powerful vise, "the jaws of which couldn't be got nearer than two inches to each other." Holmes's words may have a deeper sting than Harlan deserved, but Holmes's basic judgment seems correct.

HARLAN, J., dissenting.

The opinion in these cases proceeds, as it seems to me, upon grounds entirely too narrow and artificial. The substance and spirit of the recent amendments of the constitution have been sacrificed by a subtle and ingenious verbal criticism. "It is not the words of the law but the internal sense of it that makes the law. The letter of the law is the body; the sense and reason of the law is the soul." Constitutional provisions, adopted in the interest of liberty, and for the purpose of securing, through national legislation, if need be, rights inhering in a state of freedom, and belonging to American citizenship, have been so construed as to defeat the ends the people desired to accomplish, which they attempted to accomplish, and which they supposed they had accomplished by changes in their fundamental law. By this I do not mean that the determination of these cases should have been materially controlled by considerations of mere expediency or policy. I mean only, in this form, to express an earnest conviction that the court has departed from the familiar rule requiring, in the interpretation of constitutional provisions, that full effect be given to the intent with which they were adopted.

The purpose of the first section of the act of congress of March 1, 1875, was to prevent race discrimination. It does not assume to define the general conditions and limitations under which inns, public conveyances, and places of public amusement may be conducted, but only declares that such conditions and limitations, whatever they may be, shall not be applied, by way of discrimination, on account of race, color, or previous condition of servitude. The second section provides a penalty against any one denying, or aiding or inciting the denial, to any citizen that equality of right given by the first section, except for reasons by law applicable to citizens of every race or color, and regardless of any previous condition of servitude.

There seems to be no substantial difference between my brethren and myself as to what was the purpose of congress; for they say that the essence of the law is, not to declare broadly that all persons shall be entitled to the full and equal enjoyment of the accommodations, advantages, facilities, and privileges of inns, public conveyances, and theaters, but that such enjoyment shall not be subject to any conditions applicable only to citizens of a particular race or color, or who had been in a previous condition of servitude. The effect of the statute, the court says, is that colored citizens, whether formerly slaves or not, and citizens of other races, shall have the same accommodations and privileges in all inns, public conveyances, and places of amusement as are enjoyed by white persons, and vice versa.

The court adjudges that congress is without power, under either the thirteenth or fourteenth amendment, to establish such regulations, and that the first and second sections of the statute are, in all their parts, unconstitutional and void. . . .

The terms of the thirteenth amendment are absolute and universal. They embrace every race which then was, or might thereafter be, within the United States. No race, as such, can be excluded from the benefits or rights thereby conferred. Yet it is historically true that that amendment was suggested by the condition, in this country, of that race which had been declared by this court to have had, according to the opinion entertained by the most civilized portion of the white race at the time of the adoption of the constitution, "no rights which the white man was bound to respect," none of the privileges or immunities secured by that instrument to citizens of the United States. It had reference, in a peculiar sense, to a people which (although the larger part of them were in slavery) had been invited by an act of congress to aid, by their strong right arms, in saving from overthrow a government which, theretofore, by all of its departments, had treated them as an inferior race, with no legal rights or privileges except such as the white race might choose to grant them.

These are the circumstances under which the thirteenth amendment was proposed for adoption. They are now recalled only that we may better understand what was in the minds of the people when that amendment was being considered, and what were the mischiefs to be remedied, and the grievances to be redressed. . . .

The thirteenth amendment, my brethren concede, did

something more than to prohibit slavery as an institution, resting upon distinctions of race, and upheld by positive law. They admit that it established and decreed universal civil freedom throughout the United States. But did the freedom thus established involve nothing more than exemption from actual slavery? Was nothing more intended than to forbid one man from owning another as property? Was it the purpose of the nation simply to destroy the institution, and then remit the race, theretofore held in bondage, to the several states for such protection, in their civil rights, necessarily growing out of freedom, as those states, in their discretion, choose to provide? Were the states, against whose solemn protest the institution was destroyed, to be left perfectly free, so far as national interference was concerned, to make or allow discriminations against that race, as such, in the enjoyment of those fundamental rights that inhere in a state of freedom? . . .

That there are burdens and disabilities which constitute badges of slavery and servitude, and that the express power delegated to congress to enforce, by appropriate legislation, the thirteenth amendment, may be exerted by legislation of a direct and primary character, for the eradication, not simply of the institution, but of its badges and incidents, are propositions which ought to be deemed indisputable. They lie at the very foundation of the civil rights act of 1866. Whether that act was fully authorized by the thirteenth amendment alone, without the support which it afterwards received from the fourteenth amendment, after the adoption of which it was re-enacted with some additions, the court, in its opinion, says it is unnecessary to inquire. But I submit, with all respect to my brethren, that its constitutionality is conclusively shown by other portions of their opinion. It is expressly conceded by them that the thirteenth amendment established freedom; that there are burdens and disabilities, the necessary incidents of slavery, which constitute its substance and visible form; that congress, by the act of 1866, passed in view of the thirteenth amendment, before the fourteenth was adopted, undertook to remove certain burdens and disabilities, the necessary incidents of slavery, and to secure to all citizens of every race and color, and without regard to previous servitude, those fundamental rights which are the essence of civil freedom, namely, the same right to make and enforce contracts, to sue, be parties, give evidence, and to inherit, purchase, lease, sell, and convey property as is enjoyed by white citizens; that under the thirteenth amendment congress has to do with slavery and its incidents; and that legislation, so far as necessary or proper to eradicate all forms and incidents of slavery and involuntary servitude, may be direct and primary, operating upon the acts of individuals, whether sanctioned by state legislation or not. These propositions being conceded, it is impossible, as it seems to me, to question the constitutional validity of the civil rights act of 1866. I do not contend that the thirteenth amendment invests congress with authority, by legislation, to regulate the entire body of the civil rights which citizens enjoy, or may enjoy, in the several states. But I do hold that since slavery, as the court has repeatedly declared, was the moving or principal cause of the adoption of that amendment, and since that institution rested wholly upon the inferiority, as a race, of those held in bondage, their freedom necessarily involved immunity from, and protection against, all discrimination against them, because of their race, in respect of such civil rights as belong to freemen of other races. Congress, therefore, under its express power to enforce that amendment, by appropriate legislation, may enact laws to protect that people against the deprivation, on account of their race, of any civil rights enjoyed by other freemen in the same state; and such legislation may be of a direct and primary character, operating upon states, their officers and agents, and also upon, at least, such individuals and corporations as exercise public functions and wield power and authority under the state. . . .

What has been said is sufficient to show that the power of congress under the thirteenth amendment is not necessarily restricted to legislation against slavery as an institution upheld by positive law, but may be exerted to the extent at least of protecting the race, so liberated, against discrimination, in respect of legal rights belonging to freemen, where such discrimination is based upon race. . . .

Congress has not, in these matters, entered the domain of state control and supervision. It does not assume to prescribe the general conditions and limitations under which inns, public conveyances, and places of public amusement shall be conducted or managed. It simply declares in effect that since the nation has established universal freedom in this country for all time, there shall be no discrimination, based merely upon race or color, in respect of the legal rights in the accommodations and advantages of public conveyances, inns, and places of public amusement.

I am of opinion that such discrimination is a badge of servitude, the imposition of which congress may prevent under its power, through appropriate legislation, to enforce the thirteenth amendment; and consequently, without reference to its enlarged power under the fourteenth amendment, the act of March 1, 1875, is not, in my judgment, repugnant to the constitution.

It remains now to consider these cases with reference to the power congress has possessed since the adoption of the fourteenth amendment.

Before the adoption of the recent amendments it had become, as we have seen, the established doctrine of this court that negroes, whose ancestors had been imported and sold as slaves, could not become citizens of a state, or even of the

United States, with the rights and privileges guarantied to citizens by the national constitution; further, that one might have all the rights and privileges of a citizen of a state without being a citizen in the sense in which that word was used in the national constitution, and without being entitled to the privileges and immunities of citizens of the several states. Still further, between the adoption of the thirteenth amendment and the proposal by congress of the fourteenth amendment, on June 16, 1866, the statute-books of several of the states, as we have seen, had become loaded down with enactments which, under the guise of apprentice, vagrant, and contract regulations, sought to keep the colored race in a condition, practically, of servitude. It was openly announced that whatever rights persons of that race might have as freemen, under the guaranties of the national constitution, they could not become citizens of a state, with the rights belonging to citizens, except by the consent of such state; consequently, that their civil rights, as citizens of the state, depended entirely upon state legislation. To meet this new peril to the black race, that the purposes of the nation might not be doubted or defeated, and by way of further enlargement of the power of congress, the fourteenth amendment was proposed for adoption. . . .

But when, under what circumstances, and to what extent may congress, by means of legislation, exert its power to enforce the provisions of this amendment? The logic of the opinion of the majority of the court—the foundation upon which its whole reasoning seems to rest—is that the general government cannot, in advance of hostile state laws or hostile state proceedings, actively interfere for the protection of any of the rights, privileges, and immunities secured by the fourteenth amendment. It is said that such rights, privileges, and immunities are secured by way of prohibition against state laws and state proceedings affecting such rights and privileges, and by power given to congress to legislate for the purpose of carrying such prohibition into effect; also, that congressional legislation must necessarily be predicated upon such supposed state laws or state proceedings, and be directed to the correction of their operation and effect.

In illustration of its position, the court refers to the clause of the constitution forbidding the passage by a state of any law impairing the obligation of contracts. The clause does not, I submit, furnish a proper illustration of the scope and effect of the fifth section of the fourteenth amendment. No express power is given congress to enforce, by primary direct legislation, the prohibition upon state laws impairing the obligation of contracts. Authority is, indeed, conferred to enact all necessary and proper laws for carrying into execution the enumerated powers of congress, and all other powers vested by the constitution in the government of the United States, or in any department or officer thereof. And, as heretofore shown, there is also, by necessary implication, power in congress, by legislation, to protect a right derived from the national constitution. But a prohibition upon a state is not a power in congress or in the national government. It is simply a denial of power to the state. And the only mode in which the inhibition upon state laws impairing the obligation of contracts can be enforced, is, indirectly, through the courts, in suits where the parties raise some question as to the constitutional validity of such laws. The judicial power of the United States extends to such suits, for the reason that they are suits arising under the constitution. The fourteenth amendment presents the first instance in our history of the investiture of congress with affirmative power, by legislation, to enforce an express prohibition upon the states. It is not said that the judicial power of the nation may be exerted for the enforcement of that amendment. No enlargement of the judicial power was required, for it is clear that had the fifth section of the fourteenth amendment been entirely omitted, the judiciary could have stricken down all state laws and nullified all state proceedings in hostility to rights and privileges secured or recognized by that amendment. The power given is, in terms, by congressional legislation, to enforce the provisions of the amendment. . . .

But what was secured to colored citizens of the United States—as between them and their respective states—by the grant to them of state citizenship? With what rights, privileges, or immunities did this grant from the nation invest them? There is one, if there be no others—exemption from race discrimination in respect of any civil right belonging to citizens of the white race in the same state. That, surely, is their constitutional privilege when within the jurisdiction of other states. And such must be their constitutional right, in their own state, unless the recent amendments be "splendid baubles," thrown out to delude those who deserved fair and generous treatment at the hands of the nation. Citizenship in this country necessarily imports equality of civil rights among citizens of every race in the same state. It is fundamental in American citizenship that, in respect of such rights, there shall be no discrimination by the state, or its officers, or by individuals, or corporations exercising public functions or authority, against any citizen because of his race or previous condition of servitude. . . .

If, then, exemption from discrimination in respect of civil rights is a new constitutional right, secured by the grant of state citizenship to colored citizens of the United States, why may not the nation, by means of its own legislation of a primary direct character, guard, protect, and enforce that right? It is a right and privilege which the nation conferred. It did not come from the states in which those colored citizens reside. . . .

The opinion of the court, as I have said, proceeds upon the

ground that the power of congress to legislate for the protection
of the rights and privileges secured by the fourteenth amendment cannot be brought into activity except with the view, and
as it may become necessary, to correct and annul state laws and
state proceedings in hostility to such rights and privileges. In
the absence of state laws or state action, adverse to such rights
and privileges, the nation may not actively interfere for their
protection and security. Such I understand to be the position of
my brethren. If the grant to colored citizens of the United
States of citizenship in their respective states imports exemption from race discrimination, in their states, in respect of the
civil rights belonging to citizenship, then, to hold that the
amendment remits that right to the states for their protection,
primarily, and stays the hands of the nation, until it is assailed
by state laws or state proceedings, is to adjudge that the amendment, so far from enlarging the powers of congress,—as we
have heretofore said it did,—not only curtails them, but reverses the policy which the general government has pursued
from its very organization. Such an interpretation of the
amendment is a denial to congress of the power, by appropriate
legislation, to enforce one of its provisions. In view of the circumstances under which the recent amendments were incorporated into the constitution, and especially in view of the
peculiar character of the new rights they created and secured, it
ought not to be presumed that the general government has ab-
dicated its authority, by national legislation, direct and primary
in its character, to guard and protect privileges and immunities
secured by that instrument. Such an interpretation of the constitution ought not to be accepted if it be possible to avoid it. Its
acceptance would lead to this anomalous result: that whereas,
prior to the amendments, congress, with the sanction of this
court, passed the most stringent laws—operating directly and
primarily upon states, and their officers and agents, as well as

upon individuals—in vindication of slavery and the right of the master, it may not now, by legislation of a like primary and direct character, guard, protect, and secure the freedom established, and the most essential right of the citizenship granted, by the constitutional amendments. I venture, with all respect for the opinion of others, to insist that the national legislature may, without transcending the limits of the constitution, do for human liberty and the fundamental rights of American citizenship, what it did, with the sanction of this court, for the protection of slavery and the rights of the masters of fugitive slaves. If fugitive slave laws, providing modes and prescribing penalties whereby the master could seize and recover his fugitive slave, were legitimate exertions of an implied power to protect and enforce a right recognized by the constitution, why shall the hands of congress be tied, so that—under an express power, by appropriate legislation, to enforce a constitutional provision, granting citizenship—it may not, by means of direct legislation, bring the whole power of this nation to bear upon states and their officers, and upon such individuals and corporations exercising public functions, as assume to abridge, impair, or deny rights confessedly secured by the supreme law of the land?

It does not seem to me that the fact that, by the second clause of the first section of the fourteenth amendment, the states are expressly prohibited from making or enforcing laws abridging the privileges and immunities of citizens of the United States, furnishes any sufficient reason for holding or maintaining that the amendment was intended to deny congress the power, by general, primary, and direct legislation, of protecting citizens of the United States, being also citizens of their respective states, against discrimination, in respect to their rights as citizens, founded on race, color, or previous condition of servitude. Such an interpretation of the amendment is plainly repugnant to its fifth section, conferring upon congress power, by appropriate legislation, to enforce, not merely the provisions containing prohibitions upon the states, but all of the provisions of the amendment, including the provisions, express and implied, of the grant of citizenship in the first clause of the first section of the article. This alone is sufficient for holding that congress is not restricted to the enactment of laws adapted to counteract and redress the operation of state legislation, or the action of state officers of the character prohibited by the amendment. It was perfectly well known that the great danger to the equal enjoyment by citizens of their rights, as citizens, was to be apprehended, not altogether from unfriendly state legislation, but from the hostile action of corporations and individuals in the states. And it is to be presumed that it was intended, by that section, to clothe congress with power and authority to meet that danger. If the rights intended to be secured by the act of 1875 are such as belong to the citizen, in common or equally with other citizens in the same state, then it is not to be denied that such legislation is appropriate to the end which congress is authorized to accomplish, viz., to protect the citizen, in respect of such rights, against discrimination on account of his race. As to the prohibition in the fourteenth amendment upon the making or enforcing of state laws abridging the privileges of citizens of the United States, it was impossible for any state to have enforced laws of that character. The judiciary could have annulled all such legislation under the provision that the constitution shall be the supreme law of the land, anything in the constitution or laws of any state to the contrary notwithstanding. The states were already under an implied prohibition not to abridge any privilege or immunity belonging to citizens of the United States as such. Consequently, the prohibition upon state laws hostile to the rights belonging to citizens of the United States, was intended only as an express limitation on the powers of the states, and was not intended to diminish, in the slightest degree, the authority which the nation has always exercised, of protecting, by means of its own direct legislation, rights created or secured by the constitution. The purpose not to diminish the national authority is distinctly negatived by the express grant of power, by legislation, to enforce every provision of the amendment, including that which, by the grant of citizenship in the state, secures exemption from race discrimination in respect of the civil rights of citizens.

It is said that any interpretation of the fourteenth amendment different from that adopted by the court, would authorize congress to enact a municipal code for all the states, covering every matter affecting the life, liberty, and property of the citizens of the several states. Not so. Prior to the adoption of that amendment the constitutions of the several states, without, perhaps, an exception, secured all persons against deprivation of life, liberty, or property, otherwise than by due process of law, and, in some form, recognized the right of all persons to the equal protection of the laws. These rights, therefore, existed before that amendment was proposed or adopted. If, by reason of that fact, it be assumed that protection in these rights of persons still rests, primarily, with the states, and that congress may not interfere except to enforce, by means of corrective legislation, the prohibitions upon state laws or state proceedings inconsistent with those rights, it does not at all follow that privileges which have been granted by the nation may not be protected by primary legislation upon the part of congress. The rights and immunities of persons recognized in the prohibitive clauses of the amendments were always under the protection, primarily, of the states, while rights created by or derived from the United States have always been, and, in the nature of things, should always be, primarily, under the protection of the general government. Exemption from race discrimination in respect of the civil rights which are fundamental in citizenship in a republican government, is, as we have seen, a new constitutional right, created by the nation, with express power in congress, by legislation, to enforce the constitutional provision from which it is derived. If, in some sense, such race discrimination is a denial of the equal protection of the laws, within the letter of the last clause of the first section, it cannot be possible that a mere prohibition upon state denial of such equal protection to persons within its jurisdiction, or a prohibition upon state laws abridging the privileges and immunities of citizens of the United States, takes from the nation the power which it has uniformly exercised of protecting, by primary direct legislation, those privileges and immunities which existed under the constitution before the adoption of the fourteenth amendment, or which have been created by that amendment in behalf of those thereby made citizens of their respective states. It was said of *Dred Scott v. Sandford* that this court in that case overruled the action of two generations, virtually inserted a new clause in the constitution, changed its character, and made a new departure in the workings of the federal government. I may be permitted to say that if the recent amendments are so construed that congress may not, in its own discretion, and independently of the action or non-action of the states, provide, by legislation of a primary and direct character, for the security of rights created by the national constitution; if it be adjudged that the obligation to protect the fundamental privileges and immunities granted by the fourteenth amendment to citizens residing in the several states, rests, primarily, not on the nation, but on the states; if it be further adjudged that individuals and corporations exercising public functions may, without liability to direct primary legislation on the part of congress, make the race of citizens the ground for denying them that equality of civil rights which the constitution ordains as a principle of republican citizenship,—then, not only the foundations upon which the national supremacy has always securely rested will be materially disturbed, but we shall enter upon an era of constitutional law when the rights of freedom and American citizenship cannot receive from the nation that efficient protection which heretofore was accorded to slavery and the rights of the master.

But if it were conceded that the power of congress could not be brought into activity until the rights specified in the act of 1875 had been abridged or denied by some state law or state action, I maintain that the decision of the court is erroneous. There has been adverse state action within the fourteenth amendment as heretofore interpreted by this court. . . .

In every material sense applicable to the practical enforcement of the fourteenth amendment, railroad corporations, keepers of inns, and managers of places of public amusement are agents of the state, because amenable, in respect of their public duties and functions, to public regulation. It seems to me that . . . a denial by these instrumentalities of the state to the citizen, because of his race, of that equality of civil rights secured to him by law, is a denial by the state within the meaning of the fourteenth amendment. If it be not, then that race is left, in respect of the civil rights under discussion, practically at the mercy of corporations and individuals wielding power under public authority.

But the court says that congress did not, in the act of 1866, assume, under the authority given by the thirteenth amendment, to adjust what may be called the social rights of men and races in the community. I agree that government has nothing to do with social, as distinguished from technically legal, rights of individuals. No government ever has brought, or ever can bring, its people into social intercourse against their wishes. Whether one person will permit or maintain social relations with another is a matter with which government has no con-

cern. I agree that if one citizen chooses not to hold social intercourse with another, he is not and cannot be made amenable to
the law for his conduct in that regard; for no legal right of a citizen is violated by the refusal of others to maintain merely social
relations with him, even upon grounds of race. What I affirm is
that no state, nor the officers of any state, nor any corporation
or individual wielding power under state authority for the public benefit or the public convenience, can, consistently either
with the freedom established by the fundamental law, or with
that equality of civil rights which now belongs to every citizen,
discriminate against freemen or citizens, in their civil rights,
because of their race, or because they once labored under disabilities imposed upon them as a race. The rights which congress, by the act of 1875, endeavored to secure and protect are
legal, not social, rights. The right, for instance, of a colored citizen to use the accommodations of a public highway upon the
same terms as are permitted to white citizens is no more a social
right than his right, under the law, to use the public streets of a
city, or a town, or a turnpike road, or a public market, or a post-
office, or his right to sit in a public building with others, of
whatever race, for the purpose of hearing the political questions
of the day discussed. Scarcely a day passes without our seeing in
this court-room citizens of the white and black races sitting side
by side watching the progress of our business. It would never
occur to any one that the presence of a colored citizen in a
court-house or court-room was an invasion of the social rights
of white persons who may frequent such places. And yet such a
suggestion would be quite as sound in law—I say it with all respect—as is the suggestion that the claim of a colored citizen to
use, upon the same terms as is permitted to white citizens, the
accommodations of public highways, or public inns, or places
of public amusement, established under the license of the law,
is an invasion of the social rights of the white race....

My brethren say that when a man has emerged from slavery, and by the aid of beneficent legislation has shaken off the inseparable concomitants of that state, there must be some stage in the progress of his elevation when he takes the rank of a mere citizen, and ceases to be the special favorite of the laws, and when his rights as a citizen, or a man, are to be protected in the ordinary modes by which other men's rights are protected. It is, I submit, scarcely just to say that the colored race has been the special favorite of the laws. What the nation, through congress, has sought to accomplish in reference to that race is, what had already been done in every state in the Union for the white race, to secure and protect rights belonging to them as freemen and citizens; nothing more. The one underlying purpose of congressional legislation has been to enable the black race to take the rank of mere citizens. The difficulty has been to compel a recognition of their legal right to take that rank, and to secure the enjoyment of privileges belonging, under the law, to them as a component part of the people for whose welfare and happiness government is ordained. At every step in this direction the nation has been confronted with class tyranny, which a contemporary English historian says is, of all tyrannies, the most intolerable, "for it is ubiquitous in its operation, and weighs, perhaps, most heavily on those whose obscurity or distance would withdraw them from the notice of a single despot." To-day it is the colored race which is denied, by corporations and individuals wielding public authority, rights fundamental in their freedom and citizenship. At some future time it may be some other race that will fall under the ban. If the constitutional amendments be enforced, according to the intent with which, as I conceive, they were adopted, there cannot be, in this republic, any class of human beings in practical subjection to another class, with power in the latter to dole out to the former just such privileges as they may choose to grant. The supreme law of the land has decreed that no authority shall be exercised in this country upon the basis of discrimination, in respect of civil rights, against freemen and citizens because of their race, color, or previous condition of servitude. To that decree—for the due enforcement of which, by appropriate legislation, congress has been invested with express power—every one must bow, whatever may have been, or whatever now are, his individual views as to the wisdom or policy, either of the recent changes in the fundamental law, or of the legislation which has been enacted to give them effect.

For the reasons stated I feel constrained to withhold my assent to the opinion of the court.

⚜   ⚜   ⚜

Justice Harlan's dissent is as impassioned about slavery and freedom as any in the Supreme Court reports except perhaps some by Justice Thurgood Marshall, the Court's first African American member. Justice Harlan's verbose opinion would have allowed Congress to enact civil rights legislation. What effects would that have had?

Justice Harlan's opinion has three themes. First, the Civil Rights Act of 1875 is addressed to slavery's legacy, and is within the power given Congress in the Thirteenth Amendment. The power is one over the "badges and incidents" of slavery, and so would not cover much of what we now think of as civil rights —discrimination against women or against persons with disabilities, for example. Perhaps more important, Justice Harlan would have acknowledged *power* in Congress, but nothing guaranteed that Congress would exercise that power. The Civil Rights Act of 1875 was the last spasm of political support for the South's reconstruction. As noted earlier, in 1876 a compromise placed Rutherford B. Hayes in the White House in exchange for the withdrawal of federal troops from the South. Neither in Washington nor in the South was there ongoing political support for civil rights. And, when African Americans obtained enough political power to generate support for new civil rights legislation, they could work around the *Civil Rights Cases* by invoking Congress's power to regulate commerce among the states as the constitutional basis for civil rights legislation (see Chapter 8). Justice Harlan's dissent might have provided a more satisfying basis for that legislation—a moral one rather than one appealing to commerce—but civil rights legislation in the twentieth century did not openly advert to Justice Harlan's dissent.

And, perhaps most important, having a civil rights statute on the books is no guarantee that African Americans would have experienced civil equality. Not only would they have to have enough resources to bring cases, but in addition they would have to persuade judges and juries that their rights had indeed been violated. Businesses that did not want to serve African Americans could have come up with excuses for their actions, describing those denied service as "rowdy" or "drunken," for example, and many juries would have accepted those excuses. Such cases did occasionally arise in states that had local laws prohibiting discrimination in rail service, and juries did indeed sometimes accept the railroads' explanations. When businesses offered this type of explanation, they could defeat a claim that they had discriminated *on the basis of race,* which is all the statute reached. And, they could do so even if Justice Harlan's argument that railroads were instruments of the government had been accepted.

Justice Harlan's other themes indicate the limited protection his dissent would have given African Americans. Like others of his time, he insisted on a distinction between civil rights and social rights. Congress could protect civil rights under the

Fourteenth Amendment, but not social rights. In Justice Harlan's world, the category of civil rights was fundamental but narrow. Its most important component was the right to enter into contracts. When a business opened its doors and invited patrons to enter, the patrons had a civil right to accept the invitation—to make a contract to buy what the business was offering. If Congress chose, it could require businesses to fill their end of the bargain and allow African Americans to patronize the businesses on the same terms whites did.

Justice Harlan's dissent might have been read even more narrowly. Accepting at least conditionally the requirement that the Fourteenth Amendment kicked in only when there was state action, Justice Harlan would have found such action in state regulations granting corporations charters to operate and imposing conditions on their operation. The Civil Rights Act of 1875 was not a general nondiscrimination statute. It applied only to inns, common carriers, and places of public accommodation. As the majority pointed out, nearly all the businesses covered by the statute were extensively regulated already—and, indeed, in most states were under a legal duty to accept all comers. Perhaps Justice Harlan's dissent might have been confined to extensively regulated businesses.

And, finally, lurking underneath all of this was Justice Harlan's agreement that Congress did not have the power to enforce what he and his contemporaries called social rights. The most notable of these was the right to choose one's associates. The boundaries between social rights and civil rights were never all that clear, and the Court's decision in the *Civil Rights Cases* reduced the pressure to draw the lines precisely. Suppose African Americans did have a civil right to buy a ticket to a play. Could the theater owner require that they sit in a separate section of the theater? Today we would say that such a requirement was just as much a violation of civil rights as the refusal to sell the ticket. In the 1880s, a powerful argument could have been made that the theater owner violated only the *social* right to choose one's associates. Similar arguments might have been made about requiring nondiscrimination in employment, where people worked side-by-side, and even about *laws* requiring segregation in public areas, which would have been defended as methods of protecting the social rights of whites to choose their associates (see Chapter 5).

Of course Justice Harlan's opinion *could* be read more broadly. The category of civil rights could have expanded, that of social rights narrowed. That indeed happened in the twentieth century, to the point where we now have difficulty understanding why anything might justify violating something we agree is a civil right. The acknowledgement of congressional power to protect the rights guaranteed by the Fourteenth Amendment might have encouraged the courts to do so as well, by expansive readings of congressional legislation. That happened, too, after and probably because of the civil rights movement of the 1950s and 1960s. In itself, though, Justice Harlan's dissent made some outcomes possible that the majority foreclosed. It did not guarantee that actual outcomes would be different.

CHAPTER 5

"There is no caste here."

Plessy v. Ferguson, 1896

The compromise of 1876 that placed Rutherford B. Hayes in the White House halted progress in overcoming the legacy of slavery, and over the next decade race relations in the South gradually worsened. Informal restrictions on where blacks could go or live were widespread, but it was not until the late 1880s that these and similar restrictions began to harden into law.

In 1890 the Louisiana legislature enacted an early Jim Crow law requiring that whites and blacks ride in separate—but "equal"—railroad cars. The railroads were not happy with this statute, because it increased their costs of operating trains, and of course neither were Louisiana's African Americans. A group in New Orleans organized to bring a test case challenging the statute. Homer Plessy, one of whose great-grandparents was black (and so Plessy was classified as "black" under Louisiana's law), agreed to serve as the lead plaintiff.

Plessy was represented by a then famous author Albion Tourgee, who argued that Louisiana's statute violated the Fourteenth Amendment's guarantee of equal protection of the laws. The Supreme Court disagreed. The Fourteenth Amendment protected only "civil" rights and not "social" rights: "[I]n the nature of things, it could not have been intended to abolish distinctions based upon color, or to enforce social, as distinguished from political, equality, or a commingling of the two races upon terms unsatisfactory to either of them." These categories were reasonably well established in the constitutional discourse of the nineteenth century. Civil rights included the rights to own property and make contracts; social rights included the right of association. Because Louisiana did not deny Plessy the right to make *some* contract with the railroad by buying a ticket, and because the statute limited both whites and blacks equally, the segregation statute did not violate Plessy's civil rights.

Again, according to the Court, the segregation statute did not "necessarily imply the inferiority of either race to the other." It was a "fallacy," Justice Brown wrote, to assume that enforced segregation "stamps the colored race with a badge of inferiority. If this be so, it is not by reason of anything found in the act, but solely because the colored race chooses to put that construction upon it." Plessy's arguments also "assume that social prejudices may be overcome by legislation," but that was false. Laws are "powerless to eradicate racial instincts. . . . If one race be inferior to the other socially, the constitution of the United States cannot put them upon the same plane."

As in the *Civil Rights Cases,* Justice Harlan was the only dissenter.

⚜   ⚜   ⚜

MR. JUSTICE HARLAN, dissenting. . . .

In respect of civil rights, common to all citizens, the Constitution of the United States does not, I think, permit any public authority to know the race of those entitled to be protected in the enjoyment of such rights. Every true man has pride of race, and under appropriate circumstances when the rights of others, his equals before the law, are not to be affected, it is his privilege to express such pride and to take such action based upon it as to him seems proper. But I deny that any legislative body or judicial tribunal may have regard to the race of citizens when the civil rights of those citizens are involved. Indeed, such legislation, as that here in question, is inconsistent not only with that equality of rights which pertains to citizenship, National and State, but with the personal liberty enjoyed by every one within the United States. . . .

These notable additions to the fundamental law [the Thirteenth, Fourteenth, and Fifteenth amendments] were welcomed by the friends of liberty throughout the world. They removed the race line from our governmental systems. They had, as this court has said, a common purpose, namely, to secure "to a race recently emancipated, a race that through many generations have been held in slavery, all the civil rights that the superior race enjoy." They declared, in legal effect, this court has further said, "that the law in the States shall be the same for the black as for the white; that all persons, whether colored or white, shall stand equal before the laws of the States, and, in regard to the colored race, for whose protection the amendment was primarily designed, that no discrimination shall be made against them by law because of their color." We also said: "The words of the amendment, it is true, are prohibitory, but they contain a necessary implication of a positive immunity, or right, most valuable to the colored race—the right to exemption from unfriendly legislation against them distinctively as colored—exemption from legal discriminations, implying inferiority in civil society, lessening the security of their enjoyment of the rights which others enjoy, and discriminations which are steps towards reducing them to the condition of a subject race." It was, consequently, adjudged that a state law that excluded

citizens of the colored race from juries, because of their race and
however well qualified in other respects to discharge the duties
of jurymen, was repugnant to the Fourteenth Amendment....

It was said in argument that the statute of Louisiana does
not discriminate against either race, but prescribes a rule applicable alike to white and colored citizens. But this argument
does not meet the difficulty. Every one knows that the statute in
question had its origin in the purpose, not so much to exclude
white persons from railroad cars occupied by blacks, as to exclude colored people from coaches occupied by or assigned to
white persons. Railroad corporations of Louisiana did not
make discrimination among whites in the matter of accommodation for travellers. The thing to accomplish was, under the
guise of giving equal accommodation for whites and blacks, to
compel the latter to keep to themselves while travelling in railroad passenger coaches. No one would be so wanting in candor
as to assert the contrary. The fundamental objection, therefore,
to the statute is that it interferes with the personal freedom of
citizens. "Personal liberty," it has been well said, "consists in the
power of locomotion, of changing situation, or removing one's
person to whatsoever places one's own inclination may direct,
without imprisonment or restraint, unless by due course of
law." [From William Blackstone's *Commentaries on the Laws,*
written in England in the late eighteenth century and enormously influential among American lawyers through the nineteenth century.] If a white man and a black man choose to
occupy the same public conveyance on a public highway, it is
their right to do so, and no government, proceeding alone on
grounds of race, can prevent it without infringing the personal
liberty of each.

It is one thing for railroad carriers to furnish, or to be required by law to furnish, equal accommodations for all whom
they are under a legal duty to carry. It is quite another thing for

government to forbid citizens of the white and black races from travelling in the same public conveyance, and to punish officers of railroad companies for permitting persons of the two races to occupy the same passenger coach. If a State can prescribe, as a rule of civil conduct, that whites and blacks shall not travel as passengers in the same railroad coach, why may it not so regulate the use of the streets of its cities and towns as to compel white citizens to keep on one side of a street and black citizens to keep on the other? Why may it not, upon like grounds, punish whites and blacks who ride together in street cars or in open vehicles on a public road or street? Why may it not require sheriffs to assign whites to one side of a court-room and blacks to the other? And why may it not also prohibit the commingling of the two races in the galleries of legislative halls or in public assemblages convened for the considerations of the political questions of the day? Further, if this statute of Louisiana is consistent with the personal liberty of citizens, why may not the State require the separation in railroad coaches of native and naturalized citizens of the United States, or of Protestants and Roman Catholics? . . .

The white race deems itself to be the dominant race in this country. And so it is, in prestige, in achievements, in education, in wealth and in power. So, I doubt not, it will continue to be for all time, if it remains true to its great heritage and holds fast to the principles of constitutional liberty. But in view of the Constitution, in the eye of the law, there is in this country no superior, dominant, ruling class of citizens. There is no caste here. Our Constitution is color-blind, and neither knows nor tolerates classes among citizens. In respect of civil rights, all citizens are equal before the law. The humblest is the peer of the most powerful. The law regards man as man, and takes no account of his surroundings or of his color when his civil rights as guaranteed by the supreme law of the land are involved. It is, therefore, to be regretted that this high tribunal, the final expositor of the fundamental law of the land, has reached the conclusion that it is competent for a State to regulate the enjoyment by citizens of their civil rights solely upon the basis of race.

In my opinion, the judgment this day rendered will, in time, prove to be quite as pernicious as the decision made by this tribunal in the Dred Scott case. . . . The recent amendments of the Constitution, it was supposed, had eradicated these principles from our institutions. But it seems that we have yet, in some of the States, a dominant race—a superior class of citizens, which assumes to regulate the enjoyment of civil rights, common to all citizens, upon the basis of race. The present decision, it may well be apprehended, will not only stimulate aggressions, more or less brutal and irritating, upon the admitted rights of colored citizens, but will encourage the belief that it is possible, by means of state enactments, to defeat the beneficent purposes which the people of the United States had in view when they adopted the recent amendments of the Constitution, by one of which the blacks of this country were made citizens of the United States and of the States in which they respectively reside, and whose privileges and immunities, as citizens, the States are forbidden to abridge. Sixty millions of whites are in no danger from the presence here of eight millions of blacks. The destinies of the two races, in this country, are indissolubly linked together, and the interests of both require that the common government of all shall not permit the seeds of race hate to be planted under the sanction of law. What can more certainly arouse race hate, what more certainly create and perpetuate a feeling of distrust between these races, than state enactments, which, in fact, proceed on the ground that colored citizens are so inferior and degraded that they cannot be allowed to sit in public coaches occupied by white citizens? That, as all will admit, is the real meaning of such legislation as was enacted in Louisiana.

The sure guarantee of the peace and security of each race is the clear, distinct, unconditional recognition by our governments, National and State, of every right that inheres in civil freedom, and of the equality before the law of all citizens of the United States without regard to race. State enactments, regulating the enjoyment of civil rights, upon the basis of race, and cunningly devised to defeat legitimate results of the war, under the pretence of recognizing equality of rights, can have no other result than to render permanent peace impossible, and to keep alive a conflict of races, the continuance of which must do harm to all concerned. This question is not met by the suggestion that social equality cannot exist between the white and black races in this country. That argument, if it can be properly regarded as one, is scarcely worthy of consideration; for social equality no more exists between two races when travelling in a passenger coach or a public highway than when members of the same races sit by each other in a street car or in the jury box, or stand or sit with each other in a political assembly, or when they use in common the streets of a city or town, or when they are in the same room for the purpose of having their names placed on the registry of voters, or when they approach the ballot-box in order to exercise the high privilege of voting.

There is a race so different from our own that we do not permit those belonging to it to become citizens of the United States. Persons belonging to it are, with few exceptions, absolutely excluded from our country. I allude to the Chinese race. But by the statute in question, a Chinaman can ride in the same passenger coach with white citizens of the United States, while citizens of the black race in Louisiana, many of whom, perhaps, risked their lives for the preservation of the Union, who are entitled, by law, to participate in the political control of the State and nation, who are not excluded, by law or by reason of their race, from public stations of any kind, and who have all the legal rights that belong to white citizens, are yet declared to be criminals, liable to imprisonment, if they ride in a public coach occupied by citizens of the white race. It is scarcely just to say that a colored citizen should not object to occupying a public coach assigned to his own race. He does not object, nor, perhaps, would he object to separate coaches for his race, if his rights under the law were recognized. But he objects, and ought never to cease objecting to the proposition, that citizens of the white and black races can be adjudged criminals because they sit, or claim the right to sit, in the same public coach on a public highway. . . .

If evils will result from the commingling of the two races upon public highways established for the benefit of all, they will be infinitely less than those that will surely come from state legislation regulating the enjoyment of civil rights upon the basis of race. We boast of the freedom enjoyed by our people above all other peoples. But it is difficult to reconcile that boast with a state of the law which, practically, puts the brand of servitude and degradation upon a large class of our fellow-citizens, our equals before the law. The thin disguise of "equal" accommodations for passengers in railroad coaches will not mislead any one, nor atone for the wrong this day done. . . .

I am of opinion that the statute of Louisiana is inconsistent with the personal liberty of citizens, white and black, in that State, and hostile to both the spirit and letter of the Constitution of the United States. If laws of like character should be enacted in the several States of the Union, the effect would be in the highest degree mischievous. Slavery, as an institution tolerated by law would, it is true, have disappeared from our country, but there would remain a power in the States, by sinister legislation, to interfere with the full enjoyment of the blessings of freedom; to regulate civil rights, common to all citizens, upon the basis of race; and to place in a condition of legal inferiority a large body of American citizens, now constituting a part of the political community called the People of the United States, for whom, and by whom through representatives, our government is administered. Such a system is inconsistent with the guarantee given by the Constitution to each State of a republican form of government, and may be stricken down by Congressional action, or by the courts in the discharge of their solemn duty to maintain the supreme law of the land, anything in the constitution or laws of any State to the contrary notwithstanding.

⚜   ⚜   ⚜

In the *Civil Rights Cases,* businesses wanted to discriminate among their patrons, and Congress tried to stop them. In *Plessy,* the railroads did not want to discriminate among their patrons, believing that doing so would be more expensive than operating a single class of service for all train riders, and the state legislature forced them to discriminate. Justice Harlan again argued that the Constitution—here, by its own force and without any supporting congressional legislation—protected African Americans' civil right to enter into contracts with willing sellers, the railroads.

Would segregation have disappeared if Justice Harlan's opinion had prevailed? Not necessarily. He argued only *if* whites and blacks chose to associate, the state could not prevent them from doing so. Nothing would prevent whites from choosing to sit only in "white-only" railroad cars, or from pressuring railroads to offer such cars—and nothing would prevent the railroads from giving in to such pressure if they thought they would lose more by trying to operate unsegregated cars than by operating segregated ones. What Justice Harlan's opinion would have done is foreclose *state-mandated* segregation. The domain of that form of segregation was not unimportant, of course: segregated courtrooms sent a strong message to African Americans that the white community regarded them as inferior.

The Court's decision in *Plessy* encouraged the spread of legally mandated segregation, which had already begun to take hold in the South. Its most important manifestation was probably in segregated schools. Would Justice Harlan's opinion have meant that the South could not maintain segregated schools? The answer is complicated. Southern support for public education, never strong, might have been even weaker if schools had to be integrated. Perhaps the costs to white children and to businesses would have eventually led to the expansion of public schools in the South, but the immediate effect probably would have been the development of private schools for white children and a sharp reduction in public support for schools for African American children. Requiring that schools be integrated might have encouraged an even more rapid move to "voluntary" residential segregation coupled with neighborhood schools—a fairly easy course in cities, a more difficult one in rural areas where residential segregation was hard to achieve.

Justice Harlan's opinion did not rule out an additional possibility: that legally mandated segregation in some settings, including public education, might protect a social right rather than infringe on a civil right. The idea, later articulated by the noted constitutional scholar Herbert Wechsler, is that public education involved public compulsion, not individual choice. Requiring segregation on the railroads, as Justice Harlan said, interfered with the rights of whites and blacks to "choose to occupy the same public conveyance." Children in public schools had no choice about which school to attend. Segregated public education might be said to protect the social right of whites (and African Americans?) to choose their associates. (Technically, I suppose, Southern states would have to provide several sets of schools—one for whites who did not want to associate with African Americans, one for the African Americans excluded from those schools but open to whites, and perhaps one for African Americans who did not want to associate with whites. I have no doubt that ingenious minds would have been able to explain why Southern states did not have to *allow* whites to attend schools open to African Americans.)

Justice Harlan's powerful statement, "Our Constitution is color-blind," has been taken to support claims that public affirmative action programs, which do take race into account, are unconstitutional. It does, but there is more in Justice Harlan's opinion than that phrase. The immediately preceding sentence, "There is no caste here," and other phrases in the opinion suggest that Justice Harlan was concerned about laws that made one race "dominant" over others or that assumed that one race was "inferior and degraded"—characterizations that can be applied only with some difficulty to affirmative action programs. Like all great opinions, Justice Harlan's is open to interpretation, its meaning depending on what later readers want to make of it.

Finally, though to Justice Harlan the Constitution may have been color-blind, the society he described—and he himself—were hardly that. He seemed bothered by the fact that people from China living in Louisiana could ride in the cars reserved for whites even though they were not eligible for citizenship, while African Americans, who were citizens, could not. It is not hard to feel some racism in that concern. And Justice Harlan expected "the white race" to remain dominant in the country—

socially, but not legally. Today's vision of civil rights is more expansive. Social subordination seems to many just as much a problem for our society as legal subordination does. For many today, the idea of civil rights for all entails the elimination of social subordination, too. Whether Justice Harlan's more limited vision is preferable to that is open to dispute.

CHAPTER 6

"Room for debate and for an honest difference of opinion."

Lochner v. New York, 1905

The industrial revolution arrived in force in the United States after the Civil War. One effect was dislocation caused by periodic economic booms and busts. Another was the growth of labor unions. Workers used their unions both to attempt to bargain collectively with employers, and to get legislatures to enact "protective" labor laws—statutes regulating workplace conditions and setting maximum hours of and minimum wages for work. State legislatures could use what were called their traditional "police powers" to justify enacting laws dealing with health and safety. Under the constitutional theory prevailing in the late nineteenth century, maximum hours laws were harder to justify. The problem was that they had no direct connection to safety and health, and that they prevented some workers from signing contracts to work extra hours for extra pay. Constitutional theory allowed legislatures to step in if there was some special reason to think that the workers were not really signing the contracts voluntarily, but standard constitutional theory would not allow legislatures to assume that workers in *every* industry were coerced into working extra hours. The constitutional hook for this concern was the due process clause. According to proponents of mainstream constitutional theory, that clause's guarantee that a person's liberty would not be taken away without due process of law protected a "liberty of contract" against unjustified or arbitrary regulation. This interpretation, which went by the seemingly self-contradictory name *substantive due process,* actually had a long history in Anglo-American law; scholars have traced its roots to Magna Carta in 1215, and the idea had been sporadically invoked to strike down economic regulations as arbitrary from the mid-1800s on.

The bakery industry in New York was divided into two sectors—large commercial bakeries that operated essentially around the clock, and smaller bakeries that were open for shorter periods. The large bakeries could schedule work in shifts, but the smaller ones had to have their workers on hand throughout the day. Operating on small profit margins, the smaller bakeries also cut corners when it came to keeping the workplace safe—not simply for their workers, but in failing to make sure that the bread they produced was not contaminated.

The workers in New York's larger bakeries were organized and lobbied in the state legislature for the adoption of a comprehensive statute regulating bakeries. After several years of struggle under the leadership of Henry Weissmann, and with the help of newspaper articles exposing the ways in which bad working conditions in smaller bakeries led to the presence of contaminated bread in markets, they persuaded the state legislature in 1895 to adopt a statute dealing with health and safety issues in bakeries—and also setting a limit of ten hours per day for six days a week on how long any worker could work at a bakery. The statute was usually referred to as the "Ten Hour Law," but Justice Harlan's dissent calls it, equally accurately, a "sixty-hours" law.

The state's larger bakeries could live with the Ten Hour Law, but smaller bakeries suffered. Joseph Lochner owned a small bakery in Utica, New York. After he was fined $50 for violating the ten-hour law, Lochner challenged the statute's constitutionality. Among his lawyers, ironically, was Henry Weissmann, who had left the labor movement to open his own bakery.

The U.S. Supreme Court agreed with Lochner. The question, Justice Rufus Peckham wrote, was, "Is this a fair, reasonable and appropriate exercise of the police power of the State, or is it an unreasonable, unnecessary and arbitrary interference with the right of the individual to his personal liberty or to enter into those contracts in relation to labor which may seem to him appropriate or necessary for the support of himself and his family?" The Court did not see how there was any real connection between working no more than ten hours and protecting the health and safety of workers, much less between the hours limitation and ensuring that the bread that was produced was safe for consumers. (Lochner had not violated, and did not challenge, the provisions in the statute that were clearly related to health and safety.) "Clean and wholesome bread does not depend upon whether the baker works but ten hours a day...."

Nor could the Court see why bakeries were any different from other workplaces: upholding the Ten Hour Law, the Court said, would mean that legislatures could prevent workers in every industry from agreeing to work extra hours.

The Court knew that the health justifications for the statute were hardly the ones bakery workers cared about. Workers saw maximum hours laws as a way of redistributing some of the fruits of their labor—their employers' profits—to themselves. But, Justice Peckham wrote, considering the statute as "a labor law, pure and simple," there was no reason to think that redistribution was justified. Bakery employees were no more exploited than any other workers, nor were "bakers as a class..."

[un]equal in intelligence and capacity to men in other trades." They could "assert their rights and care for themselves" in their bargaining with their employers.

Four justices dissented, in two separate opinions.

⚜   ⚜   ⚜

MR. JUSTICE HARLAN, with whom MR. JUSTICE WHITE and MR. JUSTICE DAY concurred, dissenting....

I take it to be firmly established that what is called the liberty of contract may, within certain limits, be subjected to regulations designed and calculated to promote the general welfare or to guard the public health, the public morals or the public safety....

Granting then that there is a liberty of contract which cannot be violated even under the sanction of direct legislative enactment, but assuming, as according to settled law we may assume, that such liberty of contract is subject to such regulations as the State may reasonably prescribe for the common good and the well-being of society, what are the conditions under which the judiciary may declare such regulations to be in excess of legislative authority and void? Upon this point there is no room for dispute; for, the rule is universal that a legislative enactment, Federal or state, is never to be disregarded or held invalid unless it be, beyond question, plainly and palpably in excess of legislative power.... If there be doubt as to the validity of the statute, that doubt must therefore be resolved in favor of its validity, and the courts must keep their hands off, leaving the legislature to meet the responsibility for unwise legislation. If the end which the legislature seeks to accomplish be one to which its power extends, and if the means employed to that end, although not the wisest or best, are yet not plainly and palpably unauthorized by law, then the court cannot interfere. In other words, when the validity of a statute is questioned, the burden of proof, so to speak, is upon those who assert it to be unconstitutional....

It is plain that this statute was enacted in order to protect the physical well-being of those who work in bakery and confectionery establishments. It may be that the statute had its origin, in part, in the belief that employers and employees in such establishments were not upon an equal footing, and that the necessities of the latter often compelled them to submit to such exactions as unduly taxed their strength. Be this as it may, the statute must be taken as expressing the belief of the people of New York that, as a general rule, and in the case of the average man, labor in excess of sixty hours during a week in such establishments may endanger the health of those who thus labor. Whether or not this be wise legislation it is not the province of the court to inquire. Under our systems of government the courts are not concerned with the wisdom or policy of legislation. So that in determining the question of power to interfere with liberty of contract, the court may inquire whether the means devised by the State are germane to an end which may be lawfully accomplished and have a real or substantial relation to the protection of health, as involved in the daily work of the persons, male and female, engaged in bakery and confectionery establishments. But when this inquiry is entered upon I find it impossible, in view of common experience, to say that there is here no real or substantial relation between the means employed by the State and the end sought to be accomplished by its legislation....

Professor Hirt in his treatise on the "Diseases of the Workers" has said: "The labor of the bakers is among the hardest and most laborious imaginable, because it has to be performed under conditions injurious to the health of those engaged in it. It is hard, very hard work, not only because it requires a great deal

of physical exertion in an overheated workshop and during unreasonably long hours, but more so because of the erratic demands of the public, compelling the baker to perform the
greater part of his work at night thus depriving him of an opportunity to enjoy the necessary rest and sleep, a fact which is
highly injurious to his health." Another writer says: "The constant inhaling of flour dust causes inflammation of the lungs
and of the bronchial tubes. The eyes also suffer through this
dust, which is responsible for the many cases of running eyes
among the bakers. The long hours of toil to which all bakers are
subjected produce rheumatism, cramps and swollen legs. The
intense heat in the workshops induces the workers to resort to
cooling drinks, which together with their habit of exposing the
greater part of their bodies to the change in the atmosphere,
is another source of a number of diseases of various organs.
Nearly all bakers are pale-faced and of more delicate health
than the workers of other crafts, which is chiefly due to their
hard work and their irregular and unnatural mode of living,
whereby the power of resistance against disease is greatly di-
minished. The average age of a baker is below that of other
workmen; they seldom live over their fiftieth year, most of them
dying between the ages of forty and fifty. During periods of epidemic diseases the bakers are generally the first to succumb to
the disease, and the number swept away during such periods
far exceeds the number of other crafts in comparison to the
men employed in the respective industries. When, in 1720, the
plague visited the city of Marseilles, France, every baker in
the city succumbed to the epidemic, which caused considerable
excitement in the neighboring cities and resulted in measures
for the sanitary protection of the bakers." ...

    We judicially know that the question of the number of
hours during which a workman should continuously labor has
been, for a long period, and is yet, a subject of serious consider-

ation among civilized peoples, and by those having special knowledge of the laws of health. Suppose the statute prohibited labor in bakery and confectionery establishments in excess of eighteen hours each day. No one, I take it, could dispute the power of the State to enact such a statute. But the statute before us does not embrace extreme or exceptional cases. It may be said to occupy a middle ground in respect of the hours of labor. What is the true ground for the State to take between legitimate protection, by legislation, of the public health and liberty of contract is not a question easily solved, nor one in respect of which there is or can be absolute certainty. There are very few, if any, questions in political economy about which entire certainty may be predicated....

I do not stop to consider whether any particular view of this economic question presents the sounder theory. What the precise facts are it may be difficult to say. It is enough for the determination of this case, and it is enough for this court to know, that the question is one about which there is room for debate and for an honest difference of opinion. There are many reasons of a weighty, substantial character, based upon the experience of mankind, in support of the theory that, all things considered, more than ten hours' steady work each day, from week to week, in a bakery or confectionery establishment, may endanger the health, and shorten the lives of the workmen, thereby diminishing their physical and mental capacity to serve the State, and to provide for those dependent upon them....

MR. JUSTICE HOLMES, dissenting.

I regret sincerely that I am unable to agree with the judgment in this case, and that I think it my duty to express my dissent.

This case is decided upon an economic theory which a large

part of the country does not entertain. If it were a question whether I agreed with that theory I should desire to study it further and long before making up my mind. But I do not conceive that to be my duty, because I strongly believe that my agreement or disagreement has nothing to do with the right of a majority to embody their opinions in law. It is settled by various decisions of this court that state constitutions and state laws may regulate life in many ways which we as legislators might think as injudicious or if you like as tyrannical as this, and which equally with this interfere with the liberty to contract. Sunday laws and usury laws are ancient examples. A more modern one is the prohibition of lotteries. The liberty of the citizen to do as he likes so long as he does not interfere with the liberty of others to do the same, which has been a shibboleth for some well-known writers, is interfered with by school laws, by the Post Office, by every state or municipal institution which takes his money for purposes thought desirable, whether he likes it or not. The Fourteenth Amendment does not enact Mr. Herbert Spencer's Social Statics. The other day we sustained the Massachusetts vaccination law. The decision sustaining an eight hour law for miners is still recent. Some of these laws embody convictions or prejudices which judges are likely to share. Some may not. But a constitution is not intended to embody a particular economic theory, whether of paternalism and the organic relation of the citizen to the State or of *laissez faire.* It is made for people of fundamentally differing views, and the accident of our finding certain opinions natural and familiar or novel and even shocking ought not to conclude our judgment upon the question whether statutes embodying them conflict with the Constitution of the United States.

General propositions do not decide concrete cases. The decision will depend on a judgment or intuition more subtle than any articulate major premise. But I think that the proposition just stated, if it is accepted, will carry us far toward the end. Every opinion tends to become a law. I think that the word liberty in the Fourteenth Amendment is perverted when it is held to prevent the natural outcome of a dominant opinion, unless it can be said that a rational and fair man necessarily would admit that the statute proposed would infringe fundamental principles as they have been understood by the traditions of our people and our law. It does not need research to show that no such sweeping condemnation can be passed upon the statute before us. A reasonable man might think it a proper measure on the score of health. Men whom I certainly could not pronounce unreasonable would uphold it as a first instalment of a general regulation of the hours of work. Whether in the latter aspect it would be open to the charge of inequality I think it unnecessary to discuss.

⚜ ⚜ ⚜

The Court's decision in *Lochner* gave its name to an entire period in constitutional history. According to the usual story, during the *Lochner* era the Supreme Court did in fact enforce as constitutional law something like a strong theory of laissez faire, invalidating numerous Progressive-era laws aimed at improving working conditions. In this story, a world in which the dissenting opinions had prevailed would have been quite different from what happened in the United States in the first decades of the twentieth century. Progressive initiatives would have taken root rather than being stymied. Workers and consumers would have had safer workplaces and safer products to consume. The reforms associated with the New Deal might have been introduced more gradually. Perhaps the Great Depression might have been avoided.

So the story goes. The reality is as usual more complicated.

The Supreme Court during the *Lochner* era was hardly as retrograde as the conventional account has it. Indeed, rather than striking down consumer and worker protection laws willy-nilly, the Court routinely upheld them. It drew the line, though, at laws regulating the wages and hours of ordinary workers, as in *Lochner* itself. Perhaps the most controversial applications of this approach were decisions invalidating efforts to impose minimum wage and maximum hours rules for "child labor"—defined to cover children sometimes younger than ten years old. A great deal of consumer and worker protection legislation survived the tests created by the majority in *Lochner*.

Justices Harlan and Holmes offer slightly different approaches to the constitutional question. Justice Harlan returns us to the approach suggested by Judge Gibson in *Eakin v. Raub* (Chapter 1). He would have upheld the maximum hours law as a measure, not to make sure that bakers earned a decent living, but to protect their health. He acknowledged that the evidence of its effectiveness in doing so was subject to some dispute, but, he argued, the maximum hours law should be upheld if people could reasonably think that it made sense as a health measure. Justice Holmes's approach was slightly more radical. He too ultimately treated the maximum hours law as a health measure, but along the way he expressed greater skepticism than Justice Harlan about whether the Constitution protected a general liberty to contract. Instead, he would have deferred to "dominant opinion," which is to say, he would have upheld any statute that did not "infringe fundamental principles" found in "the traditions of our people and our law." And, in his concluding sentences, he asserted that it would not be unreasonable to regulate workers' hours as such, that is, without worrying about whether doing so improved their health.

Would the maximum hours law actually have improved the well-being of bakers? On the score of health, probably not.

Working in a bakery might not be a particularly healthy occupation, because of the possibility of inhaling flour dust—although it is not clear that it was any less healthy than many other occupations. But allowing bakers to work for ten hours a day but not twelve probably would not have had much effect on their health. What about their general well-being? Here the problem is that at least some bakers *wanted* to work the extra hours, to get the additional pay that they could then use on things they valued—education for their children, for example.

The economics of maximum hours laws are complicated. Most economists agree that sometimes maximum hours laws (and what are economically equivalent, minimum wage laws) improve the general conditions of workers even if they prevent some workers from earning as much money as they could. Most economists think that the circumstances in which this general improvement occurs are quite rare, and that in general workers as a class are better off if each worker can negotiate a package of wages and hours that satisfies both the worker and the employer. That belief, though, may be as much a matter of faith as of empirical truth, which returns us to the perspectives offered by the *Lochner* dissents: what should the courts do when reasonable people disagree about the economic or health effects of legislation?

The *Lochner* era lasted only a few decades, and the dissents were vindicated when the Supreme Court upheld a host of statutes enacted during the New Deal and after (see Chapter 9). *Lochner* may have imposed some costs on society between 1905 and 1937, but those costs may not have been large. It seems fantastic to believe that holding it unconstitutional to regulate wages and hours somehow caused the Great Depression, although several Supreme Court justices endorsed that view in explaining why it was appropriate to overrule *Lochner* but not *Roe v. Wade*.

And, perhaps most important, the repudiation of *Lochner* suggests that, in Justice Holmes's terms, "dominant opinion" will eventually have its way—at least if it remains dominant for long enough. That should caution us against overestimating the importance of Supreme Court decisions. Perhaps those decisions might sometimes weaken a "dominant" opinion to the point where it disappears and the Court's view prevails. Remember, though, that *Dred Scott*—and perhaps *Lochner*—did much to *strengthen* the political position of those who rejected the Court's opinion. At the very least, whether a Court decision matters, except in the very short run, requires us to look closely at the political, economic, and social forces that pushed the legislation that eventually came to the Supreme Court's attention.

CHAPTER 7

"Men feared witches and burned women."

Whitney v. California, 1927

Government officials never like being criticized, but often they cannot do anything about it. Sometimes, though, they try to punish their critics by claiming that the criticism is going to lead to very bad consequences: people will be persuaded to break the laws the critics challenge, or—in the most extreme case—they will start a violent revolution to overturn the existing government. These claims tend to find greater support during times of social turmoil, and in particular during war time, and even more particularly during times of war where domestic opposition to the war is relatively weak. The national government did not move against critics during the Mexican-American War in the 1840s, or during the Spanish-American War in 1898, because domestic opposition was quite substantial.

World War I was different. Shortly after the United States entered the war the Russian Revolution occurred and Russia withdrew from the war against Germany and Austria-Hungary. Radicals then began to oppose further intervention in the war, especially after the United States and its allies sent troops to Russia to support the Communists' opponents. Early in the Republic the Federalist-dominated Congress enacted a Sedition Act (1798), which made it a crime to criticize the president or his policies, but the act expired in 1800 and was not renewed until the 1917 Espionage Act made it a crime to make "false statements" with the intent "to promote the success of" the nation's enemies. A year later Congress passed a new Sedition Act, which made it a crime to "publish any disloyal... language intended to cause contempt or scorn for the government of the United States, the Constitution, or the flag." Numerous radicals were prosecuted for violating the Espionage and Sedition acts because they published pamphlets or made speeches criticizing U.S. participation in World War I or the intervention in Russia.

The Russian Revolution's success meant that concern over domestic radicalism persisted through the 1920s, especially as radicals organized political parties that eventually merged into the Communist Party of the United States. The national government deported alien radicals, but did not try to prosecute citizens. The states took up the slack, charging leading members of domestic Communist parties with violating laws prohibiting "criminal anarchy" or "criminal syndicalism," crimes that were defined in pretty much the same terms used in the federal Sedition Act.

Anita Whitney was a member of a prominent California family (one of her uncles was Supreme Court justice Stephen Field), who was also a prominent member of the Socialist Party. In 1919 she attended a national party meeting as a delegate from California. At the meeting the party split between its less radical and more radical members, the latter of whom—including Whitney—organized the Communist Labor Party. After rejecting a platform plank sponsored by Whitney that would have called for the achievement of the party's goals by lawful means, the new party adopted a platform advocating mass strikes and revolutionary mass action. Whitney remained at the convention until it concluded. She was charged with violating California's ban on criminal syndicalism.

In a relatively short opinion the Supreme Court upheld her conviction, relying on prior decisions finding that prosecuting people for conspiracies to overthrow the government, evidenced only by speech, did not violate the First Amendment.

Justice Louis Brandeis wrote a separate opinion. He drafted the opinion as a true dissent from a decision involving another radical, but that case was dismissed when the defendant died. Whitney's case had some technical difficulties; the record was confused about whether Whitney's lawyers had actually challenged the constitutionality of California's statute, and if they had not, the U.S. Supreme Court had no authority under the statutes governing its jurisdiction to reverse her conviction. This led Brandeis to concur in the Court's decision to affirm the conviction. (Whitney received a pardon from California governor Clement Calhoun Cloud shortly after the Court decision, so she never served any prison time.)

MR. JUSTICE BRANDEIS, concurring....

Despite arguments to the contrary which had seemed to me persuasive, it is settled that the due process clause of the Fourteenth Amendment applies to matters of substantive law as well as to matters of procedure. Thus all fundamental rights comprised within the term liberty are protected by the federal Constitution from invasion by the states. The right of free speech, the right to teach and the right of assembly are, of course, fundamental rights. These may not be denied or abridged. But, although the rights of free speech and assembly are fundamental, they are not in their nature absolute. Their exercise is subject to restriction, if the particular restriction proposed is required in order to protect the state from destruction or from serious injury, political, economic or moral.... It is said to be the function of the Legislature to determine whether at a particular time and under the particular circumstances the formation of, or assembly with, a society organized to advocate criminal syndicalism constitutes a clear and present danger of substantive evil; and that by enacting the law here in question the Legislature of California determined that question in the affirmative. . . . But where a statute is valid only in case certain conditions exist, the enactment of the statute cannot alone establish the facts which are essential to its validity. . . .

. . . Those who won our independence believed that the final end of the state was to make men free to develop their faculties, and that in its government the deliberative forces should prevail over the arbitrary. They valued liberty both as an end and as a means. They believed liberty to be the secret of happiness and courage to be the secret of liberty. They believed that freedom to think as you will and to speak as you think are means indispensable to the discovery and spread of political truth; that without free speech and assembly discussion would be futile; that with them, discussion affords ordinarily adequate protection against the dissemination of noxious doctrine; that the greatest menace to freedom is an inert people; that public discussion is a political duty; and that this should be a fundamental principle of the American government. They recognized the risks to which all human institutions are subject. But they knew that order cannot be secured merely through fear of punishment for its infraction; that it is hazardous to discourage thought, hope and imagination; that fear breeds repression; that repression breeds hate; that hate menaces stable government; that the path of safety lies in the opportunity to discuss freely supposed grievances and proposed remedies; and that the fitting remedy for evil counsels is good ones. Believing in the power of reason as applied through public discussion, they eschewed silence coerced by law—the argument of force in its worst form. Recognizing the occasional tyrannies of governing majorities, they amended the Constitution so that free speech and assembly should be guaranteed.

Fear of serious injury cannot alone justify suppression of free speech and assembly. Men feared witches and burnt women. It is the function of speech to free men from the bondage of irrational fears. To justify suppression of free speech there must be reasonable ground to fear that serious evil will result if free speech is practiced. There must be reasonable ground to believe that the danger apprehended is imminent. There must be reasonable ground to believe that the evil to be prevented is a serious one. Every denunciation of existing law tends in some measure to increase the probability that there will be violation of it. Condonation of a breach enhances the probability. Expressions of approval add to the probability. Propagation of the criminal state of mind by teaching syndicalism increases it. Advocacy of lawbreaking heightens it still further. But even advocacy of violation, however reprehensible morally, is not a justification for denying free speech where the advocacy falls short of incitement and there is nothing to indicate that the advocacy would be immediately acted on. The wide difference between advocacy and incitement, between preparation and attempt, between assembling and conspiracy, must be borne in mind. In order to support a finding of clear and present danger it must be shown either that immediate serious violence was to be expected or was advocated, or that the past conduct furnished reason to believe that such advocacy was then contemplated. Those who won our independence by revolution were not cowards. They did not fear political change. They did not exalt order at the cost of liberty. To courageous, self-reliant men, with confidence in the power of free and fearless reasoning applied through the processes of popular government, no danger flowing from speech can be deemed clear and present, unless the incidence of the evil apprehended is so imminent that it may befall before there is opportunity for full discussion. If there be time to expose through discussion the falsehood and fallacies, to avert the evil by the processes of education, the remedy to be applied is more speech, not enforced silence. Only an emergency can justify repression. Such must be the rule if authority is to be reconciled with freedom. Such, in my opinion, is the command of the Constitution. It is therefore always open to Americans to challenge a law abridging free speech and assembly by showing that there was no emergency justifying it.

Moreover, even imminent danger cannot justify resort to prohibition of these functions essential to effective democracy, unless the evil apprehended is relatively serious. . . . Among free men, the deterrents ordinarily to be applied to prevent crime are education and punishment for violations of the law, not abridgment of the rights of free speech and assembly. . . .

Mr. Justice Holmes joins in this opinion.

✥   ✥   ✥

Some scholars view Justice Brandeis's opinion as the greatest "dissent" in the Supreme Court Reports. It is celebrated for two main reasons. First, it develops a legal doctrine identifying the scope of the protection the First Amendment affords expression, and that doctrine eventually became the law. Earlier Justice Holmes had used a phrase—"clear and present danger" —that got at the core of limits on free speech, but Justice Brandeis's opinion elaborated that idea with an insistence that the danger be serious and, importantly, truly imminent before the government could intervene. Otherwise, the remedy for bad or dangerous speech, Justice Brandeis insisted, was more speech.

The second, and perhaps more important, reason for why

Justice Brandeis's opinion endures is its powerful rhetoric. Justice Brandeis was rarely eloquent. He had made his reputation as a man of facts and details, not of words so powerful that they captured the imagination. The *Whitney* opinion is different. Self-consciously drawing on the rhythms and some of the images in Pericles's Funeral Oration, Justice Brandeis set out an account of democracy and self-government that cannot fail to move the reader.

In many ways, Justice Brandeis's opinion in *Whitney* is the best example we have of what a dissent can do. It accurately predicts the future, and perhaps not because it anticipates some social or political change that will make its doctrine seem the right one, but because its vision of democracy and the Constitution and its rhetoric themselves contributed to making its doctrine seem correct. Few dissents combine these elements, and none as well as Justice Brandeis's opinion does.

CHAPTER 8

"Almost anything—marriage, birth, death—may in some fashion affect commerce."

National Labor Relations Board v.
Jones & Laughlin Steel Corp., 1937

Franklin Roosevelt took office in March 1933 promising Americans a New Deal that would address the nation's current economic distress and prevent future economic depressions. During the famous first one hundred days Roosevelt's administration closed the nation's banks and changed the rules on how debts had to be repaid. These policies tried to stabilize existing conditions, and by and large they worked.

Preventing future depressions called for a different set of policies, and here the New Deal floundered. Drawing on economic theories that the nation's progressives had come to hold, the administration proposed wide-ranging national economic regulation. These proposals, though, faced serious constitutional obstacles. True, the Constitution gave Congress the power to regulate "interstate" commerce, and the nation's economic system had become so integrated that almost any economic activity had some effects in other states. But the Supreme Court had given the term *commerce among the several States* a relatively narrow construction: Congress could regulate activities that "directly" affected interstate commerce, but not those that did so only indirectly; Congress could regulate transactions that crossed state lines, but not manufacturing as such (and probably not agriculture as such). Many New Deal programs ran up against these narrow constructions.

At first the programs failed the Court's constitutional test. The main challenge was to the New Deal's ill-conceived National Recovery Administration. The NRA had two main components. The first had the government authorize and then loosely supervise what were essentially industry-by-industry cartels that would set standards of fair dealing for the industry. Today, no economist would endorse such a scheme as a way of ensuring economic growth and stability, but in the 1930s progressives thought that industrial codes of conduct would damp down "destructive competition" and limit the dislocations associated with economic change.

The NRA's cartels dealt with a wide swath of the economy, and the New Deal's lawyers worried that the NRA went too far, going beyond Congress's power to regulate interstate commerce and intruding into the domain the Court had said was reserved for state regulation. They hoped to present the courts with cases showing how the NRA really did deal with large-scale economic enterprises, but they lost control of the litigation. The case that got to the Supreme Court involved a small poultry merchandiser, who bought chickens from farmers and resold them to retailers. The NRA's code of conduct for chicken sales required that merchandisers sell an entire "run" of chickens: the merchandiser had to offer all the chickens bought from a farmer, and could not pull some out of the pack because they were ill or otherwise unsuitable. The Court held that the interstate aspects of the chicken trade ended when the merchandisers bought the chickens; their resales were not part of "interstate" commerce (*A.L.A. Schechter Poultry Corp. v. United States*, 1935).

The NRA's statutory life was about to expire when the Court handed down the "sick chicken" case, and nobody was enthusiastic about renewing industrial codes of conduct. The NRA's second important element, though, was another matter. Fulfilling the legislative hopes of organized labor, the NRA required industries to bargain collectively with labor unions. New York senator Robert Wagner pushed for the adoption of a free-standing statute doing the same thing. And, again, the New Deal's lawyers worried about the Court's reaction.

The Roosevelt administration responded to these concerns along two fronts. Much more than Wagner's collective bargaining was at risk. In 1935 the Court held unconstitutional other New Deal initiatives as well, and its doctrines seemed to threaten a wide range of the administration's programs, including the new Social Security system. After winning reelection in 1936 with a strengthened Democratic majority in Congress, President Roosevelt announced a program to "reform" the Supreme Court by giving the president the power to appoint a new justice for every justice over the age of seventy-five. No one was fooled by the supposed good-government justifications for what was immediately labeled the Court-packing plan, which would have allowed Roosevelt to nominate six new justices right away. The plan ran into enormous opposition. The justices themselves denounced it, and many Democrats were worried about what they saw as Roosevelt's assault on the rule of law. Even so, the plan moved forward in the Senate, and might have been adopted. At the height of the debate, though, Senate majority leader Joseph Robinson had a fatal heart attack, and without Robinson's leadership the plan failed.

The administration's second front was simple: defend the constitutionality of the Wagner Act and other New Deal laws, using the ordinary tools lawyers had. After the New Deal's Supreme Court defeats in 1935, the administration's lawyers came to believe that they had lost partly because the challenged statutes were sloppily drafted and partly because they had not done a good job of defending them in court. They resolved to do better this time.

Careful draftsmanship and good lawyering may have helped, but luck mattered too. This time the lawyers managed to keep control over the course of litigation. Some early challenges to the Wagner Act, also known as the National Labor Relations Act, involved small operations like the Schechters'. Others, though, involved major national economic enterprises, such as the Jones & Laughlin Steel Corporation, which the Court's opinion carefully noted was the fourth largest steel producer in the country. The New Deal's opponents could readily paint the Roosevelt administration as reaching deep into areas states should regulate when it prevented the Schechters from culling their sick chickens. Explaining to the public that had elected Roosevelt that a major corporation like Jones & Laughlin was not involved in interstate commerce was far more difficult.

In the Jones & Laughlin case, the Supreme Court upheld the Wagner Act's constitutionality in an opinion written by Chief Justice Charles Evans Hughes. Roosevelt's legal team was ecstatic. Chief Justice Hughes's opinion opened by quoting detailed factual recitations in the Wagner Act, and followed with an extensive description of Jones & Laughlin's operations. The rhetorical effect was quite powerful: one would have to be a constitutional fanatic, the opinion suggested, to believe that Jones & Laughlin was not engaged in commerce among the several states. After distinguishing this case from earlier ones, Chief Justice Hughes said that "interstate commerce is a practical conception," and ended, "We are asked to shut our eyes to the plainest facts of our national life.... When industries organize themselves on a national scale, making their relation to interstate commerce the dominant factor in their activities, how can it be maintained that their industrial labor relations constitute a forbidden field into which Congress may not enter when it is necessary to protect interstate commerce from the paralyzing consequences of industrial war?"

All this was lawyerly enough. Many observers, though, believed that this and other decisions handed down in 1937 were inconsistent with existing law and resulted not from law but from Justice Owen Roberts's reaction to the Court-packing plan. Justice Roberts, who had been a railroad lawyer in Pennsylvania before his appointment to the Supreme Court, was the most moderate of the Court's conservatives. He had written some important opinions upholding New Deal-like regulations, but he had also voted with the Court's conservatives to strike down a New York minimum-wage law. In 1937 Justice Roberts voted consistently to uphold statutes that, observers suspected, he would have voted to strike down a year before. The only difference, they suggested, was that Justice Roberts had seen the Court-packing plan as a threat to the Court that could be forestalled only if the Court retreated—or became more liberal. This account always had problems with it—one of Justice Roberts's liberal votes was cast before anyone outside the White House had heard of the Court-packing plan, and others were cast after the plan seemed destined to failure in the Senate. That did not stop people from describing Justice Roberts as "the switch in time that saved nine." Justice Roberts denied that he had changed his views because of the Court-packing plan, and there are surely enough reasons grounded in law for the differences between the 1937 and the 1935 decisions to raise questions about the cynical, political view of what happened in 1937.

The justices with whom Justice Roberts had agreed earlier thought that there were no real differences between the statutes upheld in 1937 and those invalidated in 1935. The Court decided several other National Labor Relations Board (NLRB) cases on the same day it announced *Jones & Laughlin.* Just as Chief Justice Hughes made a strategic choice of a case involving a huge industrial operation as the vehicle for the Court's main opinion, the dissenters chose one of the other cases involving the Friedman-Harry Marks Clothing Company of Richmond, Virginia, a much smaller operation, as their vehicle. The dissent called on the Court to stick with its established doctrine.

ᛘ   ᛘ   ᛘ

MR. JUSTICE McREYNOLDS, dissenting.

Mr. Justice Van Devanter, Mr. Justice Sutherland, Mr. Justice Butler and I are unable to agree with the decisions just announced. . . .

In each cause the Labor Board formulated and then sustained a charge of unfair labor practices towards persons employed only in production. It ordered restoration of discharged employees to former positions with payment for losses sustained. These orders were declared invalid below upon the ground that respondents while carrying on production operations were not thereby engaging in interstate commerce; that labor practices in the course of such operations did not directly affect interstate commerce; consequently respondents' actions did not come within Congressional power. . . .

The Clothing Company is a typical small manufacturing concern which produces less than one-half of one per cent of the men's clothing produced in the United States and employs 800 of the 150,000 workmen engaged therein. If closed today, the ultimate effect on commerce in clothing obviously would be negligible. It stands alone, is not seeking to acquire a monopoly or to restrain trade. There is no evidence of a strike by its employees at any time or that one is now threatened, and nothing to indicate the probable result if one should occur. . . .

A relatively small concern caused raw material to be shipped to its plant at Richmond, Virginia, converted this into clothing, and thereafter shipped the product to points outside the state. A labor union sought members among the employees at the plant and obtained some. The Company's management opposed this effort, and in order to discourage it discharged eight who had become members. The business of the Company is so small that to close its factory would have no direct or material effect upon the volume of interstate commerce in clothing. The number of operatives who joined the union is not disclosed; the wishes of other employees are not shown; probability of a strike is not found.

The argument in support of the Board affirms: "Thus the validity of any specific application of the preventive measures of this Act depends upon whether industrial strife resulting from the practices in the particular enterprise under consideration would be of the character which Federal power could control if it occurred. If strife in that enterprise could be controlled, certainly it could be prevented."

Manifestly that view of Congressional power would extend it into almost every field of human industry. With striking lucidity, fifty years ago, *Kidd v. Pearson* declared: "If it be held that the term [commerce with foreign nations and among the several states] includes the regulation of all such manufactures as are intended to be the subject of commercial transactions in the future, it is impossible to deny that it would also include all productive industries that contemplate the same thing. The result would be that Congress would be invested, to the exclusion of the States, with the power to regulate, not only manufactures, but also agriculture, horticulture, stock raising, domestic fisheries, mining—in short, every branch of human industry." ...

Any effect on interstate commerce by the discharge of employees shown here, would be indirect and remote in the highest degree, as consideration of the facts will show. In No. 419 ten men out of ten thousand were discharged; in the other cases only a few. The immediate effect in the factory may be to create discontent among all those employed and a strike may follow, which, in turn, may result in reducing production, which ultimately may reduce the volume of goods moving in interstate commerce. By this chain of indirect and progressively remote events we finally reach the evil with which it is said the legislation under consideration undertakes to deal. A more remote and indirect interference with interstate commerce or a more definite invasion of the powers reserved to the states is difficult, if not impossible, to imagine. . . .

We are told that Congress may protect the "stream of commerce" and that one who buys raw material without the state, manufactures it therein, and ships the output to another state is in that stream. Therefore it is said he may be prevented from doing anything which may interfere with its flow.

This, too, goes beyond the constitutional limitations heretofore enforced. If a man raises cattle and regularly delivers them to a carrier for interstate shipment, may Congress prescribe the conditions under which he may employ or discharge helpers on the ranch? The products of a mine pass daily into interstate commerce; many things are brought to it from other states. Are the owners and the miners within the power of Congress in respect of the miners' tenure and discharge? May a mill owner be prohibited from closing his factory or discontinuing his business because so to do would stop the flow of products to and from his plant in interstate commerce? May employees in a factory be restrained from quitting work in a body because this will close the factory and thereby stop the flow of commerce? May arson of a factory be made a Federal offense whenever this would interfere with such flow? If the business cannot continue with the existing wage scale, may

Congress command a reduction? If the ruling of the Court just announced is adhered to these questions suggest some of the problems certain to arise....

It is gravely stated that experience teaches that if an employer discourages membership in "any organization of any kind" "in which employees participate, and which exists for the purpose in whole or in part of dealing with employers concerning grievances, labor disputes, wages, rates of pay, hours of employment or conditions of work," discontent may follow and this in turn may lead to a strike, and as the outcome of the strike there may be a block in the stream of interstate commerce. Therefore Congress may inhibit the discharge! Whatever effect any cause of discontent may ultimately have upon commerce is far too indirect to justify Congressional regulation. Almost anything—marriage, birth, death—may in some fashion affect commerce....

That Congress has power by appropriate means, not prohibited by the Constitution, to prevent direct and material interference with the conduct of interstate commerce is settled doctrine. But the interference struck at must be direct and material, not some mere possibility contingent on wholly uncertain events; and there must be no impairment of rights guaranteed....

It seems clear to us that Congress has transcended the powers granted.

⚜   ⚜   ⚜

Jones & Laughlin was one of a series of cases amounting to the so-called Constitutional Revolution of 1937. The decisions broadly validated the expansive exercises of national power initiated by Franklin D. Roosevelt's New Deal, and established the contours of the constitutional law of national power that remained substantially unchanged through the end of the twentieth century. The Rehnquist Court adjusted those contours around the margin, but the scope of national power is not substantially different today.

Some liberal constitutional scholars have attributed to conservatives a desire to restore a "Constitution in Exile." The dissent in *Jones & Laughlin* might provide an example of what the restored Constitution might look like. The dissenters can be taken as suggesting two different approaches to national power, both resting on the proposition that in a federal system like ours, national power must be limited so that people have a real chance to influence their state and local governments to adopt policies they prefer, and that might vary from one state to another. The first approach, suggested by the reference to the small number of workers who went on strike, would ask whether the national statute regulated something that had some real (or, as lawyers would put it, substantial) effects outside the state where the business was located. The second approach would distinguish between commerce, which Congress could regulate, and manufacturing and agriculture, which it could not.

These two approaches would have similar effects on national legislation dealing with working conditions, but rather different effects on national environmental legislation—both areas to which conservative constitutional theorists have directed much attention. When a manufacturing plant discharges polluted water, or emits excessive carbon dioxide into the air, its actions often have effects in other states: the water flows into a river, the carbon dioxide blows across the country. Limiting Congress's power to situations in which someone's activities had effects in other states might have small consequences for some environmental regulations; the clearest candidates are protections for quite isolated endangered species, usually insects and plants. But most of today's environmental regulation would remain constitutional under the "substantial effects" approach.

Not so if Congress could regulate only "commerce," understood to mean transactions—buying and selling—across state lines. There's nothing commercial in that sense about emitting pollution into the environment, or—in the case of agriculture—about using insecticides that run off into streams and rivers and kill fish. Returning the Constitution from exile in that form would have real consequences for contemporary environmental regulation.

Either version would severely limit existing workplace regulations—not simply regulations aimed at providing workers with safe working conditions, but even regulations dealing with pension plans. The conditions at a particular work site are precisely the kinds of local activities that the dissenters in *Jones & Laughlin* thought protected against national regulation. And, of course, workplace conditions are part of the manufacturing process—or the building process—and not part of a sales transaction across state lines.

Some of these regulations might survive as exercises of national power other than the one allowing Congress to regulate commerce. Consider, for example, antidiscrimination legislation. The *Civil Rights Cases* (Chapter 4) pushed Congress to rely on its commerce power as the basis for antidiscrimination law. And certain antidiscrimination laws, such as the ban on discrimination on the basis of race in restaurants, would still be constitutional under the Constitution returned from exile. But rules requiring nondiscrimination in employment might be put at risk. Still, Congress could rely on its power to enforce the Constitution's guarantees of equality, as Justice Harlan's dissent in the *Civil Rights Cases* argued, to support such legislation. Similarly, pension and health insurance laws might be structured around the federal tax code. All this might be so, but we would have to think about the possibility that the Constitution returned from exile would be interpreted to limit congressional power under other constitutional provisions as well.

We should note, though, that the Constitution returned from exile is, at least in this aspect, about the scope of national power. Nothing in it bars state legislatures from adopting workplace safety rules, or from adopting their own environmental protection legislation. And, indeed, throughout U.S. history, important regulatory initiatives have been tried out first at the state and local level before they were extended through national legislation. Justice Louis Brandeis extolled the division of power between state and nation as giving us the chance to use states as "laboratories" for social and economic experiments. He feared that national power—sometimes exercised by the courts, but sometimes exercised by Congress—would interfere with valuable experiments. The Constitution returned from exile might invigorate state and local governments to produce novel forms of regulation that would escape the rigidities we have come to expect from national regulation (scholars call it *ossification*), which could be extended, not by national compulsion, but as states come to emulate the successful initiatives undertaken in other states.

CHAPTER 9

"The ugly abyss of racism."

Korematsu v. United States, 1944

December 7, 1941, was, as President Roosevelt said, a date that lives in infamy. Congress declared war on the day after the Japanese military's attack on Pearl Harbor. A month after that Congress passed a statute making it a crime to violate an exclusion order. On March 24 General John DeWitt, the military commander on the West Coast, put all persons of Japanese descent, whether U.S. citizens or not, under a curfew. On May 3 General DeWitt ordered that same group to report to "Assembly Centers" in preparation for their transfer to "Relocation Centers" away from the West Coast. Eventually approximately 120,000 people were sent to these camps, of whom about 70,000 were U.S. citizens.

Military necessity was the purported justification for the creation of the detention centers, racism more likely the real one. Later reports identified no incidents of sabotage or espionage attributable to Japanese Americans, although General DeWitt incongruously claimed that the fact that no incidents occurred showed that the detention program was both successful and justified. The whole program was set against a background of widespread suspicion on the West Coast of Japanese immigrants and their citizen children. Those ordered to leave the West Coast had to abandon their homes, farms, and other property, which became available to white citizens remaining in the area. General DeWitt's final report was so clear about his racist assumptions—that everyone of Japanese origin would inevitably strongly support the nation's enemies—that lawyers in the Department of Justice struggled, with only modest success, to keep references to General DeWitt's report out of their brief to the Supreme Court.

Fred Korematsu, a U.S. citizen, grew up around San Francisco. In 1942 he had a defense-related job. When the government ordered Japanese Americans on the West Coast to report for internment, Korematsu evaded the order, moving to a new town and attempting to conceal his racial affiliation. Once discovered, he was prosecuted for refusing to report to the center from which he would be sent to the internment camps. Although the Supreme Court, upholding his conviction, seized on this detail to say that it was not really upholding the policy of holding citizens in detention camps, but only upholding the requirement that Japanese Americans report for detention, that fiction fooled no one, and the Court's decision was understood, then and since, as upholding the constitutionality of a policy of detaining U.S. citizens who had committed no crimes.

Justice Hugo Black's majority opinion began with the promising statement, "It should be noted . . . that all legal restrictions which curtail the civil rights of a single racial group are immediately suspect." But, he continued, that did not make them automatically unconstitutional, only that the courts had to give them "the most rigid scrutiny." That scrutiny, it turned out, involved a great deal of deference to the supposed military judgments made by military commanders. "Congress, reposing its confidence in this time of war in our military leaders—as inevitably it must—determined that they should have the power" to create detention camps. (Justice Black "deem[ed] it unjustifiable to call them concentration camps with all the ugly connotations that term implies.") Military commanders had been concerned about "the gravest imminent danger to the public safety." The detention centers were set up during war, and "[h]ardships are part of war, and war is an aggregation of hardships."

Three justices dissented. Two of their opinions follow.

MR. JUSTICE MURPHY, dissenting.

This exclusion of "all persons of Japanese ancestry, both alien and non-alien," from the Pacific Coast area on a plea of military necessity in the absence of martial law ought not to be approved. Such exclusion goes over "the very brink of constitutional power" and falls into the ugly abyss of racism.

In dealing with matters relating to the prosecution and progress of a war, we must accord great respect and consideration to the judgments of the military authorities who are on the scene and who have full knowledge of the military facts. The scope of their discretion must, as a matter of necessity and common sense, be wide. And their judgments ought not to be overruled lightly by those whose training and duties ill-equip them to deal intelligently with matters so vital to the physical security of the nation.

At the same time, however, it is essential that there be definite limits to military discretion, especially where martial law has not been declared. Individuals must not be left impoverished of their constitutional rights on a plea of military necessity that has neither substance nor support. Thus, like other claims conflicting with the asserted constitutional rights of the individual, the military claim must subject itself to the judicial process of having its reasonableness determined and its conflicts with other interests reconciled. "What are the allowable limits of military discretion, and whether or not they have been overstepped in a particular case, are judicial questions." (*Sterling v. Constantin*, 1932).

The judicial test of whether the Government, on a plea of military necessity, can validly deprive an individual of any of his constitutional rights is whether the deprivation is reasonably related to a public danger that is so "immediate, imminent, and impending" as not to admit of delay and not to permit the intervention of ordinary constitutional processes to alleviate the danger. Civilian Exclusion Order No. 34, banishing from a prescribed area of the Pacific Coast "all persons of Japanese ancestry, both alien and non-alien," clearly does not meet that test. Being an obvious racial discrimination, the order deprives all those within its scope of the equal protection of the laws as guaranteed by the Fifth Amendment. It further deprives these individuals of their constitutional rights to live and work where they will, to establish a home where they choose and to move about freely. In excommunicating them without benefit of hearings, this order also deprives them of all their constitutional rights to procedural due process. Yet no reasonable relation to an "immediate, imminent, and impending" public danger is evident to support this racial restriction which is one of the most sweeping and complete deprivations of constitutional rights in the history of this nation in the absence of martial law.

It must be conceded that the military and naval situation in the spring of 1942 was such as to generate a very real fear of invasion of the Pacific Coast, accompanied by fears of sabotage and espionage in that area. The military command was therefore justified in adopting all reasonable means necessary to combat these dangers. In adjudging the military action taken in light of the then apparent dangers, we must not erect too high or too meticulous standards; it is necessary only that the action have some reasonable relation to the removal of the dangers of invasion, sabotage and espionage. But the exclusion, either temporarily or permanently, of all persons with Japanese blood in their veins has no such reasonable relation. And that relation is lacking because the exclusion order necessarily must rely for its reasonableness upon the assumption that *all* persons of Japanese ancestry may have a dangerous tendency to commit sabotage and espionage and to aid our Japanese enemy in other ways. It is difficult to believe that reason, logic or experience could be marshalled in support of such an assumption.

That this forced exclusion was the result in good measure of this erroneous assumption of racial guilt rather than bona fide military necessity is evidenced by the Commanding General's Final Report on the evacuation from the Pacific Coast area. In it he refers to all individuals of Japanese descent as "subversive," as belonging to "an enemy race" whose "racial strains are undiluted," and as constituting "over 112,000 potential enemies . . . at large today" along the Pacific Coast. In support of this blanket condemnation of all persons of Japanese descent, however, no reliable evidence is cited to show that such individuals were generally disloyal, or had generally so conducted themselves in this area as to constitute a special menace to defense installations or war industries, or had otherwise by their behavior furnished reasonable ground for their exclusion as a group.

Justification for the exclusion is sought, instead, mainly upon questionable racial and sociological grounds not ordinarily within the realm of expert military judgment, supplemented by certain semi-military conclusions drawn from an unwarranted use of circumstantial evidence. Individuals of Japanese ancestry are condemned because they are said to be "a large, unassimilated, tightly knit racial group, bound to an enemy nation by strong ties of race, culture, custom and religion." They are claimed to be given to "emperor worshipping ceremonies" and to "dual citizenship." Japanese language schools and allegedly pro-Japanese organizations are cited as evidence of possible group disloyalty, together with facts as to certain persons being educated and residing at length in Japan. It is intimated that many of these individuals deliberately resided "adjacent to strategic points," thus enabling them "to carry into execution a tremendous program of sabotage on a mass scale should any considerable number of them have been inclined to do so." The need for protective custody is also asserted. The report refers without identity to "numerous incidents of violence" as well as to other admittedly unverified or cumulative incidents. From this, plus certain other events not shown to have been connected with the Japanese Americans, it is concluded that the "situation was fraught with danger to the Japanese population itself" and that the general public "was ready to take matters into its own hands." Finally, it is intimated, though not directly charged or proved, that persons of Japanese ancestry were responsible for three minor isolated shellings and bombings of the Pacific Coast area, as well as for unidentified radio transmissions and night signalling.

The main reasons relied upon by those responsible for the forced evacuation, therefore, do not prove a reasonable relation between the group characteristics of Japanese Americans and the dangers of invasion, sabotage and espionage. The reasons appear, instead, to be largely an accumulation of much of the misinformation, half-truths and insinuations that for years have been directed against Japanese Americans by people with racial and economic prejudices—the same people who have been among the foremost advocates of the evacuation. A military judgment based upon such racial and sociological considerations is not entitled to the great weight ordinarily given the judgments based upon strictly military considerations. Especially is this so when every charge relative to race, religion, culture, geographical location, and legal and economic status has been substantially discredited by independent studies made by experts in these matters.

The military necessity which is essential to the validity of the evacuation order thus resolves itself into a few intimations that certain individuals actively aided the enemy, from which it is inferred that the entire group of Japanese Americans could not be trusted to be or remain loyal to the United States. No one denies, of course, that there were some disloyal persons of Japanese descent on the Pacific Coast who did all in their power to aid their ancestral land. Similar disloyal activities have been engaged in by many persons of German, Italian and even more pioneer stock in our country. But to infer that examples of individual disloyalty prove group disloyalty and justify discriminatory action against the entire group is to deny that under our system of law individual guilt is the sole basis for deprivation of rights. Moreover, this inference, which is at the very heart of the evacuation orders, has been used in support of the abhorrent and despicable treatment of minority groups by the dictatorial tyrannies which this nation is now pledged to destroy. To give constitutional sanction to that inference in this case, however well-intentioned may have been the military command on the Pacific Coast, is to adopt one of the cruelest of the rationales used by our enemies to destroy the dignity of the individual and to encourage and open the door to discriminatory actions against other minority groups in the passions of tomorrow.

No adequate reason is given for the failure to treat these Japanese Americans on an individual basis by holding investigations and hearings to separate the loyal from the disloyal, as was done in the case of persons of German and Italian ancestry. It is asserted merely that the loyalties of this group "were unknown and time was of the essence." Yet nearly four months elapsed after Pearl Harbor before the first exclusion order was issued; nearly eight months went by until the last order was issued; and the last of these "subversive" persons was not actually removed until almost eleven months had elapsed. Leisure and deliberation seem to have been more of the essence than speed. And the fact that conditions were not such as to warrant a declaration of martial law adds strength to the belief that the factors of time and military necessity were not as urgent as they have been represented to be.

Moreover, there was no adequate proof that the Federal Bureau of Investigation and the military and naval intelligence services did not have the espionage and sabotage situation well in hand during this long period. Nor is there any denial of the fact that not one person of Japanese ancestry was accused or convicted of espionage or sabotage after Pearl Harbor while they were still free, a fact which is some evidence of the loyalty of the vast majority of these individuals and of the effectiveness of the established methods of combatting these evils. It seems incredible that under these circumstances it would have been impossible to hold loyalty hearings for the mere 112,000 persons involved—or at least for the 70,000 American citizens— especially when a large part of this number represented children and elderly men and women. Any inconvenience that may have accompanied an attempt to conform to procedural due process cannot be said to justify violations of constitutional rights of individuals.

I dissent, therefore, from this legalization of racism. Racial discrimination in any form and in any degree has no justifiable part whatever in our democratic way of life. It is unattractive in any setting but it is utterly revolting among a free people who have embraced the principles set forth in the Constitution of the United States. All residents of this nation are kin in some way by blood or culture to a foreign land. Yet they are primarily and necessarily a part of the new and distinct civilization of the United States. They must accordingly be treated at all times as the heirs of the American experiment and as entitled to all the rights and freedoms guaranteed by the Constitution.

Mr. Justice Jackson, dissenting....

Now, if any fundamental assumption underlies our system, it is that guilt is personal and not inheritable. Even if all of one's antecedents had been convicted of treason, the Constitution forbids its penalties to be visited upon him, for it provides that "no attainder of treason shall work corruption of blood, or forfeiture except during the life of the person attainted." But here is an attempt to make an otherwise innocent act a crime merely because this prisoner is the son of parents as to whom he had no choice, and belongs to a race from which there is no way to resign. If Congress in peace-time legislation should enact such a criminal law, I should suppose this Court would refuse to enforce it.

But the "law" which this prisoner is convicted of disregarding is not found in an act of Congress, but in a military order. Neither the Act of Congress nor the Executive Order of the President, nor both together, would afford a basis for this conviction. It rests on the orders of General DeWitt. And it is said that if the military commander had reasonable military grounds for promulgating the orders, they are constitutional and become law, and the Court is required to enforce them. There are several reasons why I cannot subscribe to this doctrine....

The limitation under which courts always will labor in examining the necessity for a military order are illustrated by this case. How does the Court know that these orders have a reasonable basis in necessity? No evidence whatever on that subject has been taken by this or any other court. There is sharp controversy as to the credibility of the DeWitt report. So the Court, having no real evidence before it, has no choice but to accept General DeWitt's own unsworn, self-serving statement, untested by any cross-examination, that what he did was reasonable. And thus it will always be when courts try to look into the reasonableness of a military order.

In the very nature of things, military decisions are not susceptible of intelligent judicial appraisal. They do not pretend to rest on evidence, but are made on information that often would not be admissible and on assumptions that could not be proved. Information in support of an order could not be disclosed to courts without danger that it would reach the enemy. Neither can courts act on communications made in confidence. Hence courts can never have any real alternative to accepting the mere declaration of the authority that issued the order that it was reasonably necessary from a military viewpoint.

Much is said of the danger to liberty from the Army program for deporting and detaining these citizens of Japanese extraction. But a judicial construction of the due process clause that will sustain this order is a far more subtle blow to liberty than the promulgation of the order itself. A military order, however unconstitutional, is not apt to last longer than the military emergency. Even during that period a succeeding commander may revoke it all. But once a judicial opinion rationalizes such an order to show that it conforms to the Constitution, or rather rationalizes the Constitution to show that the Constitution sanctions such an order, the Court for all time has validated the principle of racial discrimination in criminal procedure and of transplanting American citizens. The principle then lies about like a loaded weapon ready for the hand of any authority that can bring forward a plausible claim of an urgent need. Every repetition imbeds that principle more deeply in our law and thinking and expands it to new purposes. All who observe the work of courts are familiar with what Judge Cardozo described as "the tendency of a principle to expand itself to the limit of its logic." A military commander may overstep the bounds of constitutionality, and it is an incident. But if we review and approve, that passing incident becomes the doctrine of the Constitution. There it has a generative power of its own, and all that it creates will be in its own image. Nothing better illustrates this danger than does the Court's opinion in this case. . . .

Of course the existence of a military power resting on force, so vagrant, so centralized, so necessarily heedless of the individual, is an inherent threat to liberty. But I would not lead people to rely on this Court for a review that seems to me wholly delusive. The military reasonableness of these orders can only be determined by military superiors. If the people ever let command of the war power fall into irresponsible and unscrupulous hands, the courts wield no power equal to its restraint. The chief restraint upon those who command the physical forces of the country, in the future as in the past, must be their responsibility to the political judgments of their contemporaries and to the moral judgments of history.

My duties as a justice as I see them do not require me to make a military judgment as to whether General DeWitt's evacuation and detention program was a reasonable military necessity. I do not suggest that the courts should have attempted to interfere with the Army in carrying out its task. But I do not think they may be asked to execute a military expedient that has no place in law under the Constitution. I would reverse the judgment and discharge the prisoner.

⚜ ⚜ ⚜

Justice Jackson was concerned that a decision upholding the internment was both inevitable and undesirable: inevitable because the pressures of the moment forced the Court to validate what the administration had done, and undesirable because the decision would be available for future use. He may have been wrong on both counts.

Korematsu might not have been inevitable because any military necessity, real or imagined, requiring internment had passed by the time the case was decided. Indeed, on the very same day *Korematsu* was handed down, the Court ruled that those held in the detention camps who established their loyalty to the United States had to be released, a decision that amounted to a holding that the camps had to be closed in an orderly way.

And the decision turned out not to have the consequences Justice Jackson feared. Yale law professor Eugene Rostow called *Korematsu* a "disaster" in 1945, shortly after it was decided. Congress enacted the Civil Liberties Act of 1988 to provide about $20,000 in reparations to each surviving internee. Justice Murphy's denunciation of the internment as racist now appears to be the conventional wisdom, and the most notable feature of his opinion is his willingness to use the term *racist* to describe a government policy. (The term has been used in that way in the Supreme Court fewer than five times since 1945.)

Indeed, the doctrinal legacy of *Korematsu* might be said to be quite positive. The decision was the first saying that racial classifications were "suspect" and had to be given "rigid"—later the term became "strict"—scrutiny. This doctrine became the foundation of many of the central decisions vindicating claims that statutes using racial classifications violated the Constitution.

In the aftermath of the September 11, 2001, attacks, some voices were heard suggesting that interning some American citizens might again make sense. Nothing approaching such a policy was adopted. The closest approximation—a request that a large number of citizens whose national origins were in the Middle East submit to interviews with federal authorities—had none of the strongly coercive aspects of the World War II internments. Perhaps, then, Justice Murphy's dissent shows that we can learn not to make constitutional mistakes, although of course it might be that the circumstances that provoked internment have not recurred.

Justice Jackson's dissent does raise questions about judicial review that have continuing importance. Given our strong tradition that authorizes the courts to decide whether some policy is constitutional or not, what are the courts to do when they face constitutional problems where the "correct" answer cannot be given—as Justice Jackson thought was true of *Korematsu*—for fear of provoking a substantial backlash? (For an example of the backlash question, see Chapter 13.)

Justice Jackson hoped that at least sometimes the Court would be able to invoke *legal* doctrines that would allow it to duck the question, and law professor Alexander Bickel later developed a comprehensive account of what those doctrines were. They include doctrines that occasionally pop up in Court decisions today—the doctrine of "standing," which says that the courts will answer constitutional questions only when the questions are presented by people who have actually been injured by the policy they say is unconstitutional, and the "political question" doctrine, which says that the courts will not decide constitutional questions where the Constitution itself says in rather clear terms that Congress or the president has the exclusive power to do so. In 2004 the Court used one of these doctrines to avoid deciding whether the Constitution was violated by the inclusion of the words "under God" in the Pledge of Allegiance (*Elk Grove Unified School Dist. v. Newdow,* 2004). These doctrines, though, sit uncomfortably with our general tradition of judicial review, and in practice they screen out relatively few cases, almost at random, from the courts. They do not serve the ends Justice Jackson thought important to pursue.

More recently scholars have suggested that the Court can avoid backlash by constructing its decisions narrowly. The empirical evidence for that claim is thin. Another suggestion is that the Court should take the possibility of backlash into account in deciding whether the challenged policy is unconstitutional—that is, the Court should say to itself, "The very fact that we're worried about backlash if we rule this way is a reason to rule the other way." It is possible to develop a fairly esoteric story about why the possibility of backlash might properly inform constitutional interpretation, but most of the time the possibility of backlash is not going to have much to do with the usual sources judges rely on when they interpret the Constitution.

In the end, Justice Jackson probably did the right thing. Despite his desire to avoid deciding, when push came to shove, he voted on the merits and dissented, rather than ducking. And perhaps deciding rather than ducking is what judges should always do.

CHAPTER 10

"Refrain from invidious discriminations."

Goesaert v. Cleary, 1948

The Fourteenth Amendment says that every "person" is entitled to the equal protection of the laws. In the nineteenth
century, the first wave of the feminist movement tried to take
advantage of the term "person" to argue against discrimination
against women in voting and admission to the professions. The
Supreme Court treated the claims with disdain, and the
women's suffrage movement turned to the amendment process,
introducing a voting rights amendment, which became the
Nineteenth Amendment in 1920, and an equal rights amendment, which was not adopted.

Litigation against sex-based discrimination was rare as well.
In one of its few references to gender equality, the Supreme
Court defended its 1923 decision invalidating a maximum
hours law restricted to women on the ground that the adoption
of the Nineteenth Amendment showed that women were no
longer regarded by American society as different from men
(*Adkins v. Childrens Hospital,* 1923). That was plainly untrue, as
one of the Court's next encounters with sex discrimination
showed.

Goesaert v. Cleary dealt with a Michigan statute prohibiting
a woman from being a bartender (unless she was the wife or
daughter of a male bar-owner). Justice Felix Frankfurter, who as
a lawyer represented the defenders of the "protective" labor law

127

invalidated in 1923, wrote the Court's opinion upholding Michigan's law. To modern ears, the opinion's rhetoric may seem jarring. He called the subject "beguiling," and referred to the "sprightly and ribald" alewife in Shakespeare. The opinion continued, "The fact that women may now have achieved the virtues that men have long claimed as their prerogatives and now indulge in vices that men have long practiced, does not preclude the States from drawing a sharp line between the sexes, certainly, in such matters as the regulation of the liquor traffic." According to the Court, Michigan was not "play[ing] favorites among women without rhyme or reason." The state could reasonably assume that supervision of a female bartender by her husband or father would reduce the social "hazards that may confront a barmaid without such protecting oversight."

⚜   ⚜   ⚜

Mr. Justice Rutledge, with whom Mr. Justice Douglas and Mr. Justice Murphy join, dissenting.

While the equal protection clause does not require a legislature to achieve "abstract symmetry" or to classify with "mathematical nicety," that clause does require lawmakers to refrain from invidious distinctions of the sort drawn by the statute challenged in this case.

The statute arbitrarily discriminates between male and female owners of liquor establishments. A male owner, although he himself is always absent from his bar, may employ his wife and daughter as barmaids. A female owner may neither work as a barmaid herself nor employ her daughter in that position, even if a man is always present in the establishment to keep order. This inevitable result of the classification belies the assumption that the statute was motivated by a legislative solicitude for the moral and physical well-being of women who, but for the law, would be employed as barmaids. Since there could be no other conceivable justification for such discrimination against women owners of liquor establishments, the statute should be held invalid as a denial of equal protection.

⚜   ⚜   ⚜

Justice Rutledge's dissent foreshadows the path the constitutional law of sex discrimination took. He accepted the majority's doctrinal standard, that sex-based distinctions were constitutional if they were reasonable, and argued that the line Michigan drew was arbitrary and unreasonable. Ruth Bader Ginsburg, acting as a lawyer for the American Civil Liberties Union (ACLU) decades before she was appointed to the Supreme Court, developed a legal strategy to challenge sex-based discrimination that similarly accepted the "rationality" standard. She coupled that with an ingenious insight. She thought, probably correctly, that judges who were, after all, well into their sixties and beyond, might share Justice Frankfurter's skepticism about claims that women were disadvantaged by the "protections" male legislatures gave them. So, she decided, she would pick cases in which sex-based discrimination clearly disadvantaged *men.*

As others who had tried to develop strategic litigation campaigns before had already discovered, the ACLU could not completely control the pace of litigation. The first case that got to the Supreme Court did not fit into Ginsburg's strategy. An Idaho statute set up categories for people who would be given the power to administer the estates of deceased members of their families. Within each category men would be preferred over women, apparently on the theory that men were more likely to be familiar with business and financial matters than women. Sally Reed challenged the statute's operation, which would have given the power to administer the estate of her son, who had committed suicide, to her estranged husband. In a brief and unanimous opinion, the Supreme Court held the Idaho statute unconstitutional because it was unreasonable (*Reed v. Reed,* 1971).

Ginsburg's breakthrough came two years later. She represented a woman in the armed forces, who challenged a statute dealing with benefits paid to married soldiers. Every male soldier was entitled to the benefits, but female soldiers could get the benefits only if they showed that their salaries were more than half of the family's income. A fractured Supreme Court struck the statute down (*Frontiero v. Richardson,* 1973). Four justices thought that the statute was unreasonable under the existing standard. Justice William Brennan wrote for four justices, saying that the Constitution allowed sex-based discrimination only when there was a very good reason for it. The benefits statute might save a bit of money—perhaps giving benefits to all male soldiers, nearly all of whom might well make more than half of the family's income, was cheaper than asking each male solider to demonstrate that fact—but that was hardly enough to justify the distinction the statute drew, according to Justice Brennan.

Over the next decades the Court gradually moved in Justice Brennan's direction, though it never adopted the specific test he offered. In 1996, as a justice of the Supreme Court, Ruth Bader Ginsburg wrote the Court's opinion rejecting Virginia's effort to provide "separate but equal" programs of military-style "leadership training" to men and women, for men at Virginia Military Institute and for women at Mary Baldwin College (*United States v. Virginia,* 1996). Sex-based discrimination, Justice Ginsburg wrote, required "exceedingly persuasive justification," which Virginia could not supply.

The reason for the change from 1948 to 1996 is so obvious

that it does not require extended comment. Justice Frankfurter referred to "vast changes in the social and legal position of women," but the changes were even larger by 1996. A second wave of feminism swept over the country in the 1960s and after, and the Court was not immune to its effects. As a candidate for the presidency, Ronald Reagan pledged to appoint a woman to the Supreme Court, and he did so the first chance he got. Ginsburg's strategic litigation efforts helped as well. The next chapter presents an opinion in which Justice Robert Jackson says that social and political change makes legal change inevitable. The Court's sex discrimination decisions confirm his insight.

CHAPTER 11

"Our decision does not end but begins the struggle over segregation."

Brown v. Board of Education, 1954

Plessy v. Ferguson (Chapter 5) encouraged and perhaps accelerated the solidification of the South's Jim Crow system. A central feature of Jim Crow was segregation in the South's public schools. Although *Plessy* dealt with transportation and not schools, and although no Supreme Court decision ever explicitly dealt with its application to schools, everyone assumed that the decision provided a firm constitutional foundation for segregated schools.

Plessy did require that separate facilities be equal, and, in contexts outside education, the Court purported to take that requirement seriously. Starting in the 1930s, lawyers for the National Association for the Advancement of Colored People (NAACP), including Thurgood Marshall, later named to the Supreme Court, brought a series of lawsuits seeking to enforce the requirement of equality in graduate and professional schools. The Supreme Court gave this campaign a series of victories from 1938 to 1950, which encouraged Marshall and his colleagues to shift their attention to the more important targets of elementary and secondary schools.

These cases were understood to be "direct attacks" on segregation, because no one believed that the South's separate schools for African Americans were equal to those for whites, whether the measure was their physical characteristics—class sizes, up-to-date laboratories for science classes, libraries, and the like—or their more intangible qualities such as reputation in the community. Eventually, the NAACP's lawyers brought five cases to the Supreme Court—two from the border states of Delaware and Kansas, two from the deep South states of Virginia and South Carolina, and one from the District of Columbia. The cases varied in factual detail—the court in Delaware had ordered desegregation because the school facilities were not equal, the court in South Carolina found, implausibly, that a recent spate of school construction there had made the separate facilities for African Americans equal to those for whites—but they were fundamentally all the same. The question presented to the Court was whether school segregation was constitutional in a social context where achieving real equality in separate facilities was for all practical purposes impossible.

The justices struggled over what to do with the five cases. From the outset it seemed as if a majority probably would find school segregation unconstitutional, but even that was not clear. Chief Justice Fred Vinson, a Kentuckian, was at best conflicted over what to do and provided no leadership inside the Court. With an exaggerated sense of how important his contacts with Southern lawyers were, Justice Felix Frankfurter kept raising caution flags, insisting that the justices strike exactly the right tone in their opinion, and worrying about precisely what sort of remedy the Court could order if it invalidated school segregation.

It was not so much that the Court was sharply divided, but rather that the justices were at a loss to develop a coherent position, particularly because nearly all of them agreed that, if they were to invalidate segregation, the decision should be as close to unanimous as possible. The justices decided to put off deciding. To save face, they asked the lawyers to reargue the case and submit new briefs examining the background of the Fourteenth Amendment, and outlining the possible remedial orders the Court could issue.

Two important developments occurred over the summer before the second argument. Within the Court, Justice Frankfurter resolved his own ambivalences by deciding that the Court could properly put off deciding what the remedy should be. And in public, there was a dramatic change in the Court's leadership. Chief Justice Vinson died. Calling in a political chit he had earned by supporting candidate Dwight Eisenhower at a crucial point during the 1952 Republican Convention, California governor Earl Warren insisted that he get what he had been promised—an appointment to the Supreme Court when the first vacancy occurred. Although President Eisenhower and his advisers had not expected the first vacancy to be Vinson's seat, they carried through on their promise and nominated Warren to be chief justice.

Warren's arrival at the Court was decisive. Unlike his predecessor, Chief Justice Warren was firmly committed to holding segregation unconstitutional. With the leadership logjam broken, the decision after the reargument went smoothly. Chief Justice Warren decided that so important a decision had to be authored by the chief justice. He set about writing an opinion that would be short and written in terms a lay reader could understand.

The opinion Chief Justice Warren had his law clerks draft was indeed short and readable, although it left scholars of the time and since unsatisfied. After finding that the Fourteenth Amendment's history was "inconclusive" on the question of school segregation and observing that the Court could not "turn the clock back to 1868 when the Amendment was adopted, or even to 1896 when [*Plessy v. Ferguson*] was written," the opinion described education as "perhaps the most important function of state and local governments today." In a key sentence, Chief Justice Warren wrote, "To separate [African American children] from others of similar age and qualifications solely because of their race generates a feeling of inferiority as to their status in the community that may affect their hearts and minds in a way unlikely ever to be undone." A few sentences later he added a footnote citing several studies by social psychologists that, he said, provided "modern authority" for that conclusion. The opinion ended, "We conclude that in the field of public education the doctrine of 'separate but equal' has no place."

With the draft opinion in hand, Chief Justice Warren persuaded Justice Stanley Reed, who had held out against striking segregation down, to go along with the majority for the good of the nation. That left Justice Robert Jackson, who was committed to holding segregation unconstitutional, but who struggled with developing the right legal theory to justify the decision.

After the ultimate outcome was clear, Justice Jackson toyed with the idea of publishing a separate concurring opinion, and worked on it over a four-month period. He did not send the draft around to all his colleagues, but Justice Frankfurter knew it existed and, after reading it, sent Jackson a note praising the argument. Justice Jackson's law clerk E. Barrett Prettyman, later a distinguished Washington lawyer, disagreed and tried to argue Jackson out of publishing it. More influential was Chief Justice Warren. Jackson had a heart attack and was hospitalized at the end of March 1954, and, while visiting him in the hospital Warren emphasized the importance of the Court speaking in a single voice. Jackson decided not to publish his opinion, but it remained in his files.

✤   ✤   ✤

MEMORANDUM BY MR. JUSTICE JACKSON.

I.

Since the close of the Civil War, the United States has been "hesitating between two worlds—one dead, the other powerless to be born." Constitutions are easier amended than social customs, and even the North never fully conformed its racial practices to its professions.

One whose impressionable years were spent in public schools in a region where Negro pupils were very few and where economic, social and political motives united against segregating them is predisposed to the conclusion that segregation elsewhere has outlived whatever justification it may have had. The practice seems marked for early extinction. Whatever we might say today, within a generation it will be outlawed by decision of this Court because of the forces of mortality and replacement which operate upon it.

Decision of these cases would be simple if our personal opinion that school segregation is morally, economically or politically indefensible made it legally so. But it is not only established in the law of seventeen states and the national capital; it is deeply imbedded in social custom in a large part of this country. Its eradication involves nothing less than a substantial reconstruction of legal institutions and society. It persists because of fears, prides and prejudices which this Court cannot eradicate, which even in the North are latent, and occasionally ignite where the ratio of colored population to white passes a point where the latter vaguely, and perhaps unreasonably, feel themselves insecure.

However sympathetic we may be with the resentments of those who are coerced into segregation, we cannot, in considering a recasting of society by judicial fiat, ignore the claims of those who are to be coerced out of it. We cannot deny the sincerity and passion with which many feel that their blood, lineage and culture are worthy of protection by enforced separation of races and feel that they have built their segregated institutions for many years on an almost universal understanding that segregation is not constitutionally forbidden.

It has seemed almost instinctive with every race, faith, state or culture to resort to some isolating device to protect and perpetuate those qualities, real or fancied, which it especially values in itself. Separatism, either by voluntary withdrawal or by imposed segregation, has been practiced in some degree by many religions, nationalities and races, and by many—one almost can say all—governments, to alleviate tensions, prevent subversions and to quell or forestall violence. It is today being practiced on a voluntary basis by minorities, who discourage or forbid intermarriage, maintain separate denominational schools, and otherwise seek to prevent contacts which threaten dilution of blood or dissipation of faith. This instinct for self-preservation is enough to account for the prevalence of segregation in several of the Northern states.

But, in the South, the Negro appears to suffer from other antagonisms that are an aftermath of the great American white conflict. The white South harbors in historical memory, with deep resentment, the program of reconstruction and the deep humiliation of carpetbag government imposed by conquest. Whatever other motives were behind these offensive reconstruction measures and whatever their necessity or merit, the North made the Negro their emotional symbol and professed beneficiary, with the natural consequences of identifying him with all that was suffered from his Northern champions. . . .

II. DOES EXISTING LAW CONDEMN SEGREGATION?

Layman as well as lawyer must query how it is that the Constitution this morning forbids what for three-quarters of a century it has tolerated or approved. He must further speculate as to how this reversal of its meaning by the branch of the Government supposed not to make new law but only to declare existing law and which has exactly the same constitutional materials that so far as the states are concerned have existed since 1868 and in the case of the District of Columbia since 1791. Can we honestly say that the states which have maintained segregated schools have not, until today, been justified in understanding their practice to be constitutional?

Of course, for over three-quarters of a century majestic and sweeping generalities of the Due Process and Equal Protection Clauses of the Fourteenth Amendment were capable of being read to require a full and equal racial partnership in all matters within the reach of law. But neither of these Clauses specifically mentions education or segregation. Yet, if these texts had such meaning to the age that wrote them, how could the identical Due Process Clause of the Fifth Amendment for half a century have tolerated slavery in the District of Columbia? . . . Thus, there is no explicit prohibition of segregated schools and it can only be supplied by interpretation.

It is customary to turn to the original will and purpose of those responsible for adoption of a constitutional document as a basis for its subsequent interpretation. . . . [I]t was a passionate, confused and deplorable era. Like most legislative history, that of the Amendment is misleading because its sponsors played down its consequences in order to quiet fears which might cause opposition, while its opponents exaggerated the consequences to frighten away support. Among its supporters may be found a few who hoped that it would bring about com-

plete social equality and early assimilation of the liberated Negro into an amalgamated population. But I am unable to find
any indication that their support was decisi[ve], and certainly
their view had no support from the great Emancipator himself.
The majority was composed of more moderate men who appeared to be thinking in terms of ending all questions as to constitutionality of the contemporaneous statutes conferring upon
the freed man certain limited civil rights. It is hard to find an
indication that any influential body of the movement that carried the Civil War Amendments had reached the point of
thinking about either segregation or education of the Negro as
a current problem, and harder still to find that the Amendments were designed to be a solution.

If we turn from words to deeds as evidence of purpose, we
find nothing to show that the Congress which submitted these
Amendments understood or intended to prohibit the practice
here in question. The very Congress that proposed the Fourteenth Amendment, and every Congress from that day to this,
established or maintained segregated schools in the District
of Columbia, where its power over purse and policy was complete. . . .

Turning from Congress to look to the behavior of the states,
we find that equally impossible to reconcile with any understanding that the Amendment would prohibit segregation in
schools. . . .

If we look to see how judicial precedent squares with the
practice of legislators and administrators, we find that state
courts of the North and this Court, where Northern men have
predominated, have shared the understanding that these
Clauses of their own force do not prohibit the states from deciding that each race must obtain its education apart rather
than by commingling. Almost a century of decisional law rendered by judges, many of whom risked their lives for the cause

that produced these Amendments, is almost unanimous in the view that the Amendment tolerated segregation by state action, at least in the absence of congressional action to the contrary.

The custom of a people has always been recognized as a powerful lawmaker. Widespread usage has reinforced the view of legislators and educators and the opinions of the courts. This Court, in common with courts everywhere, has recognized the force of long custom and has been reluctant to use judicial power to try to recast social usages established among the people....

Convenient as it would be to reach an opposite conclusion, I simply cannot find in the conventional material of constitutional interpretation any justification for saying that in maintaining segregated schools any state or the District of Columbia can be judicially decreed, up to the date of this decision, to have violated the Fourteenth Amendment.

III. DOES THE AMENDMENT CONTEMPLATE CHANGED CONDITIONS?

The Fourteenth Amendment does not attempt to say the last word on the concrete application of its pregnant generalities. It declares that "The Congress shall have power to enforce, by appropriate legislation, the provisions of this Article." It thus makes provision for giving effect from time to time to the changes of conditions and public opinion always to be anticipated in a developing society. A policy which it outlines only comprehensively it authorized Congress to complete in detail.

If the Amendment deals at all with state segregation and education, there can be no doubt that it gives Congress a wide discretion to enact legislation on that subject binding on all states and school districts....

The futility of effect reform of our society by judicial decree is demonstrated by the history of this very matter. For many years this Court has pronounced the doctrine that, while separate facilities for each race are permissible, they must be equal. Our pronouncement to that effect has remained a dead letter in a large part of the country. Why has the separate-but-equal doctrine declared by this Court so long been a mere promise to the colored ear to be broken to the hope? . . .

I see no reason to expect a pronouncement that segregation is unconstitutional will be any more self-executing or any more sufficiently executed than our pronouncement that unequal facilities are unconstitutional. . . .

The Court can strike down legislation which supports educational segregation, but any constructive policy for abolishing it must come from Congress. Only Congress can enact a policy binding on all states and districts. . . . It can make provisions for federal funds where changes required are beyond the means of the community, for mixing the races will require extensive changes in physical plants and will impose the largest burden on some of the nation's lowest income regions. . . .

A Court decision striking down state statutes or constitutional provisions which authorize or require segregation will not produce a social transition, nor is the judiciary the agency to which the people should look for that result. Our decision may end segregation in Delaware and Kansas, because there it lingers by a tenuous lease of life. But where the practice really is entrenched, it exists independently of any statute or decision as a local usage and deep-seated custom sustained by the prevailing sentiment of the community. School districts, from habit and conviction, will carry it along without aid of state statutes. To eradicate segregation by judicial action means two generations of litigation.

It is apparent that our decision does not end but begins the struggle over segregation. . . .

IV. THE LIMITS AND BASIS OF JUDICIAL ACTION

Until today Congress has been justified in believing that segregation does not offend the Constitution. In view of the deference habitually paid by other branches of the Government to this Court's interpretation of the Constitution, it is not unlikely that a considerable part of the inertia of Congress, if not of the country, has been due to the belief that the existing system is constitutional. The necessity for judicial action on this subject arises from the doctrine concerning it which is already on our books.

It is not, in my opinion, necessary or true to say that these earlier judges, many of whom were as sensitive to human values as any of us, were wrong in their own times. With the fundamental premise that the requirement of equal protection does not disable the state from making reasonable classifications of its inhabitants nor impose the obligation to accord identical treatment to all, there can be no quarrel. . . .

But the second step in their reasoning, sometimes in reliance on precedents from slave days, sometimes from experience in their own time, was not a legal so much as a factual assumption. It was that there were differences between the Negro and the white races, viewed as a whole, such as to warrant separate classification and discrimination not only for their educational facilities but also for marriage, for access to public places of recreation, amusements or service and as passengers on common carriers and as the right to buy and own real estate.

Whether these early judges were right or wrong in their times I do not know. Certainly in the 1860's and probably throughout the Nineteenth Century the Negro population as a whole was a different people than today. Lately freed from bondage, they had little opportunity as yet to show their capacity for education or even self-support and management. There was strong belief in heredity, and the Negro's heritage was then close to primitive. Likewise, his environment from force of circumstances was not conducive to his mental development. I do not find it necessary to stigmatize as hateful or unintelligent the early assumption that Negro education presented problems that were elementary, special and peculiar and that the mass teaching of Negroes was an experiment not easily tied in with the education of pupils of more favored background. Nor, when I view the progress that was made under it, can I confidently say that the practice of each race pursuing its education apart has been, up to now, wholly to the Negro's disadvantage. My little experience in a nonsegregated school does not teach that to mingle closely with white pupils fully solves the Negro's psychological or educational problem. Indeed, Negro progress under segregation has been spectacular and, tested by the pace of history, his rise is one of the swiftest and most dramatic advances in the annals of man. It is that, indeed, which has enabled him to outgrow the system and to overcome the presumptions on which it was based.

The handicap of inheritance and environment has been too widely overcome today to warrant these earlier presumptions based on race alone. I do not say that every Negro everywhere is so advanced, nor would I know whether the proportion who have shown educational capacity is or is not in all sections similar. But it seems sufficiently general to require me to say that mere possession of colored blood, in whole or in part, no longer affords a reasonable basis for a classification for educational purposes and that each individual must be rated on his own merit. . . .

Moreover, we cannot ignore the fact that assimilation today has proceeded much beyond where it was at the earlier periods. Blush or shudder, as many will, mixture of blood has been making inroads on segregation faster than change in law. No clear line of separation between the races has been observed. More and more a large population with as much claim to white as to colored blood baffles any justice in classification for segregation.

Nor can we ignore the fact that the concept of the place of public education has markedly changed. Once a privilege conferred on those fortunate enough to take advantage of it, it is now regarded as a right of a citizen and a duty enforced by compulsory education laws. Any thought of public education as a privilege which may be given or withheld as a matter of grace has long since passed out of American thinking.

It is neither novel nor radical doctrine that statutes once held constitutional may become invalid by reason of changing conditions, and those held to be good in one state of facts may be held to be bad in another. . . .

⚜   ⚜   ⚜

Justice Jackson did not propose to dissent, making this opinion different from others in this book. It was made public only in 1988, when the questions he raised had been faced and answered, however inadequately. Yet, the opinion remains provocative.

We should put aside Justice Jackson's casual racism, except to note that neither he nor his contemporaries would have described his observations about the "progress" of African Americans in those terms, and to remind ourselves that we too may be blind to prejudices that future generations will find equally casually expressed in judicial opinions we admire today. We should put aside too the thought that Justice Jackson's opinion, had it been published in 1954, would have provided fuel for *Brown*'s opponents. True, those opponents would have seized on Justice Jackson's discussion of the inadequacy of "conventional legal materials" to support the Court's result, and would have said that it showed—from inside the Court—that the Court's decision did indeed rest on the justices' "personal opinions." Even more so had Justice Jackson adhered to his initial heading for the section, which asserted in declaratory terms that the conventional materials did not support the Court's result. The shift to the interrogative form did little to conceal Justice Jackson's conclusion. But *Brown*'s opponents were perfectly able to come up with those criticisms on their own. Southern legislators in Congress produced a "Manifesto" making Justice Jackson's points, though in less measured tones.

More interesting is Justice Jackson's effort, not terribly successful, to explain why changed conditions justified the result the Court reached. He tried to argue that the facts had changed, but his presentation was hardly convincing, and surely did not capture what made *Brown* seem correct to those who agreed with it. Notably, Justice Jackson provided no support for his judgments about the changes on which he relies. They were seat-of-the-pants judgments, which critics might even have described as "personal opinions." Chief Justice Warren's opinion for the Court was criticized for citing several social scientists as "modern authority," but at least the Chief Justice had *some* evidence to rely on. Justice Jackson had none other than his sense of the way things were.

The most interesting part of Justice Jackson's opinion is its realism. Segregation was doomed, he wrote, not because Congress would do something about it but because new justices on the Supreme Court would inevitably find it unconstitutional. And yet segregation would persist until Congress did something about it. The decisions might have some immediate effects in border states, but would have simply invited "two generations" of litigation in the deep South. In all this Justice

Jackson was basically right, although he may not have been re-alistic enough.

Desegregation did indeed proceed relatively smoothly in some border states. The deep South resisted, massively, as the phrase went. Massive resistance took advantage of the Court's faint-heartedness when it came to ordering desegregation. A year after the first *Brown* decision, the Court issued another one, dealing exclusively with what should be done. Although it would have taken little effort simply to abandon racially based school assignments, the Court did not order schools to desegre-gate in short order. Instead, it said that desegregation should start promptly and should proceed "with all deliberate speed." Here the Court equivocated. It *said* that "it should go without saying" that "disagreement" with *Brown* did not justify delay, but its refusal to insist on quick action rested on the justices' be-lief that white Southerners committed to segregation would indeed disagree with the decision and try to evade its imple-mentation.

Massive resistance involved legislation aimed at obstructing efforts by African Americans to enroll in previously white schools and, when that failed, violent opposition to desegrega-tion, and when that failed, closing public schools and opening "private" schools with government support (Chapter 13). A decade after *Brown,* few African American children in the deep South attended schools with white students.

The situation changed only when Congress intervened. The Civil Rights Act of 1964 provided that federal funds would be denied to institutions that discriminated on the basis of race. That threat became real when Congress enacted the Elemen-tary and Secondary Education Act in 1965. Before that most local schools received little or no money from the federal gov-ernment, so the threat of a funding cut-off was meaningless.

The ESEA put money on the table. The federal Department of Health, Education, and Welfare announced guidelines for determining whether a school system was moving rapidly enough toward desegregation to get federal money, and the federal courts used those guidelines to structure the remedies they awarded in the cases before them. All this meant that Southern schools began to desegregate in the mid-1960s.

By then, though, questions about what the Constitution required, which had been suppressed while the South simply refused to do anything, resurfaced. Shortly after *Brown* was decided, one prominent federal judge wrote, accurately enough, that the decision required desegregation, not integration. He meant that all *Brown* said was that school systems could not use race as the basis for assigning students to schools, not that each school had to have a racial composition similar to that in the school district as a whole. By the 1960s civil rights advocates had come to think that *Brown* did require integration. They too could draw on *Brown* to support their position.

In urban areas integration was much more difficult to achieve than desegregation. It required redrawing school assignment areas and, in the end, significant amounts of busing students from one part of a district to another. Busing remedies were extremely controversial, and became more so when *Brown* "moved North" and courts began to find that Northern school districts had engaged in racial assignment practices of a sort condemned in *Brown*. The result was, once again, resistance, and the gradual reduction in support among whites—and, in connection with busing, among some African Americans—for integration. The two-generation delay Justice Jackson foresaw had the effect of making it impossible for the federal courts to implement *Brown*. In the end, as Justice Jackson also suggested, whatever mixing of races that occurred in the United States resulted from a wider social acceptance of a multiracial and multicultural society than from the Court's interventions.

For two decades the question in the South was whether schools systems that had been segregated by law would become integrated by court order. Meanwhile, schools in the North, where segregation had not been required by law, sometimes chose as a matter of policy to seek integration—or "racial balance," as the policy's opponents often called it.

In 2007 the Supreme Court asked whether the Constitution allowed school boards to seek integration. It dealt with cases from Seattle and Louisville, where the school boards had pursued integration by occasionally assigning students to schools to achieve integration or racial balance. By then constitutional doctrine allowed race to be used as a basis for government policy—whether to burden African Americans, as segregation did, or to assist them, as proponents of integration asserted it did—only if the government was pursuing an especially important goal—"compelling" was the jargon—and could achieve that goal effectively only if race was used.

Four justices said that achieving racial balance was not a compelling goal, but five justices disagreed. Justice Anthony Kennedy, though, thought that the two school districts hadn't shown that they had to use race if they were to achieve racial balance in their schools, and so voted to strike down the policies.

Fifty-three years after *Brown,* the question of its true meaning remained a matter of controversy even after it had become an unassailable icon of constitutional law. The continuing controversy suggests that though Justice Jackson may have been wrong about what realism should tell us, he was almost certainly right that we must take a realistic view of what the Constitution can help us do about racial justice.

CHAPTER 12

"To attribute, however flatteringly, omnicompetence to judges."

Baker v. Carr, 1962

To have a representative democracy, you have to have representatives. But not just *any* system of representation: at least in the twentieth century and after, everyone would be uncomfortable with a system of representative democracy in which I got to vote for two representatives and you got to vote for only one. Some notion of equality seems implicit in the modern idea of representation. And some aspects of equality with respect to voting are indeed protected by the Constitution: the Fifteenth Amendment makes it unconstitutional to deny a person a vote because of the person's race; the Nineteenth guarantees a right to vote without regard to sex, the Twenty-Sixth does the same for people over the age of eighteen.

But there is another problem associated with representation when representatives are chosen from districts defined by geographic boundaries. You can get the equivalent of two votes for the one I have if you live in a district that has half the population of the one I live in. I am not formally denied a vote, but you have twice as good a chance as I do of making a difference in choosing who will represent the district. (Proportional representation systems do not face this problem.) Inequality in the distribution of legislative seats on the basis of a district's population seems like a denial of equality in voting rights.

The problem of malapportionment differs from other forms of denial of voting rights. After all, the person who lives in the larger district *does* get to vote, and her vote is counted and weighted equally with those of everyone else in the district. The constitutional hook for challenging malapportionment is hardly obvious either.

The best candidate is a clause providing that "the United States shall guarantee to every State in this Union a Republican Form of Government." A government in which some people get two votes, others one, might not qualify as "republican," and that might be so even if the inequality resulted from apportionment decisions rather than deliberate exclusions from the franchise. The courts are not available to enforce the guarantee clause, though. In 1849 the Supreme Court held that the clause gave the nation's political branches—Congress and the president—the duty to ensure that state governments were "republican," and not the courts (*Luther v. Borden,* 1849).

Another possibility is the Fourteenth Amendment's equal protection clause. Here too the Court's precedents were not promising. In 1946 the Supreme Court, in a divided opinion whose meaning was not entirely clear, refused to order the reapportionment of Illinois's congressional districts, where the largest district was nine times the size of the smallest (*Colegrove v. Green,* 1946). Justice Felix Frankfurter, writing the lead opinion, cautioned the courts against entering what he called the "political thicket" of apportionment. There was, he suggested, no acceptable theory that could guide the courts in deciding when an apportionment was so unequal as to violate the Constitution. Other opinions in the case suggested that the Court's refusal to act rested on special facts about the litigation in Illinois, so the possibility of renewing a Fourteenth Amendment–based challenge remained open.

Over the next decade and a half, population movement coupled with legislative inertia led to districts of such widely varying sizes that equality based challenges seemed increasingly sensible. The Supreme Court finally took up the problem in a case from Tennessee. The state's constitution required that districts be redrawn to match population changes every ten years, but the state legislature had ignored that duty since 1901. The result was that the cities of Nashville, Memphis, and Knoxville had substantially fewer representatives in proportion to their population than the state's rural districts. The Kennedy administration thought that reapportionment was a necessary part of the ideal of widening democracy to which it was committed, and supported the challenge in the Supreme Court.

After long deliberations within the Supreme Court, including an unusual second round of arguments, the Court held that the courts did indeed have a role in enforcing the idea of equal representation. Much of the majority opinion by Justice William J. Brennan was dryly technical, but its thrust was clear: the federal courts were ready to order state legislatures to redraw district boundaries to achieve greater equality in representation. What exactly that meant was left to the future.

⚜   ⚜   ⚜

Mr. Justice Frankfurter, whom Mr. Justice Harlan joins, dissenting.

The Court today reverses a uniform course of decision established by a dozen cases, including one by which the very claim now sustained was unanimously rejected only five years ago. The impressive body of rulings thus cast aside reflected the equally uniform course of our political history regarding the relationship between population and legislative representation

—a wholly different matter from denial of the franchise to individuals because of race, color, religion or sex. Such a massive repudiation of the experience of our whole past in asserting destructively novel judicial power demands a detailed analysis of the role of this Court in our constitutional scheme. Disregard of inherent limits in the effective exercise of the Court's "judicial Power" not only presages the futility of judicial intervention in the essentially political conflict of forces by which the relation between population and representation has time out of mind been and now is determined. It may well impair the Court's position as the ultimate organ of "the supreme Law of the Land" in that vast range of legal problems, often strongly entangled in popular feeling, on which this Court must pronounce. The Court's authority—possessed of neither the purse nor the sword—ultimately rests on sustained public confidence in its moral sanction. Such feeling must be nourished by the Court's complete detachment, in fact and in appearance, from political entanglements and by abstention from injecting itself into the clash of political forces in political settlements.

A hypothetical claim resting on abstract assumptions is now for the first time made the basis for affording illusory relief for a particular evil even though it foreshadows deeper and more pervasive difficulties in consequence. The claim is hypothetical and the assumptions are abstract because the Court does not vouchsafe the lower courts—state and federal—guidelines for formulating specific, definite, wholly unprecedented remedies for the inevitable litigations that today's umbrageous disposition is bound to stimulate in connection with politically motivated reapportionments in so many States. In such a setting, to promulgate jurisdiction in the abstract is meaningless. It is as devoid of reality as "a brooding omnipresence in the sky," for it conveys no intimation what relief, if any, a District Court is capable of affording that would not invite legislatures to play ducks and drakes with the judiciary. For this Court to direct the District Court to enforce a claim to which the Court has over the years consistently found itself required to deny legal enforcement and at the same time to find it necessary to withhold any guidance to the lower court how to enforce this turnabout, new legal claim, manifests an odd—indeed an esoteric—conception of judicial propriety. One of the Court's supporting opinions, as elucidated by commentary, unwittingly affords a disheartening preview of the mathematical quagmire (apart from divers judicially inappropriate and elusive determinants) into which this Court today catapults the lower courts of the country without so much as adumbrating the basis for a legal calculus as a means of extrication. Even assuming the indispensable intellectual disinterestedness on the part of judges in such matters, they do not have accepted legal standards or criteria or even reliable analogies to draw upon for making judicial judgments. To charge courts with the task of accommodating the incommensurable factors of policy that underlie these mathematical puzzles is to attribute, however flatteringly, omnicompetence to judges. The Framers of the Constitution persistently rejected a proposal that embodied this assumption and Thomas Jefferson never entertained it.

Recent legislation, creating a district appropriately described as "an atrocity of ingenuity," is not unique. Considering the gross inequality among legislative electoral units within almost every State, the Court naturally shrinks from asserting that in districting at least substantial equality is a constitutional requirement enforceable by courts. Room continues to be allowed for weighting. This of course implies that geography, economics, urban-rural conflict, and all the other non-legal factors which have throughout our history entered into political districting are to some extent not to be ruled out in the un-defined vista now opened up by review in the federal courts of state reapportionments. To some extent—aye, there's the rub. In effect, today's decision empowers the courts of the country to devise what should constitute the proper composition of the legislatures of the fifty States. If state courts should for one rea-son or another find themselves unable to discharge this task, the duty of doing so is put on the federal courts or on this Court, if State views do not satisfy this Court's notion of what is proper districting.

We were soothingly told at the bar of this Court that we need not worry about the kind of remedy a court could effec-tively fashion once the abstract constitutional right to have courts pass on a state-wide system of electoral districting is rec-ognized as a matter of judicial rhetoric, because legislatures would heed the Court's admonition. This is not only a eu-phoric hope. It implies a sorry confession of judicial impotence in place of a frank acknowledgement that there is not under our Constitution a judicial remedy for every political mischief, for every undesirable exercise of legislative power. The Framers carefully and with deliberate forethought refused so to en-throne the judiciary. In this situation, as in others of like nature, appeal for relief does not belong here. Appeal must be to an in-formed, civically militant electorate. In a democratic society like ours, relief must come through an aroused popular con-science that sears the conscience of the people's representatives. In any event there is nothing judicially more unseemly nor more self-defeating than for this Court to make in terrorem pronouncements, to indulge in merely empty rhetoric, sound-ing a word of promise to the ear, sure to be disappointing to the hope. . . .

From its earliest opinions this Court has consistently recognized a class of controversies which do not lend themselves to judicial standards and judicial remedies. To classify the various instances as "political questions" is rather a form of stating this conclusion than revealing of analysis. Some of the cases so labelled have no relevance here. But from others emerge unifying considerations that are compelling....

The influence of these converging considerations—the caution not to undertake decision where standards meet for judicial judgment are lacking, the reluctance to interfere with matters of state government in the absence of an unquestionable and effectively enforceable mandate, the unwillingness to make courts arbiters of the broad issues of political organization historically committed to other institutions and for whose adjustment the judicial process is ill-adapted—has been decisive of the settled line of cases, reaching back more than a century, which holds that Art. IV, §4, of the Constitution, guaranteeing to the States "a Republican Form of Government," is not enforceable through the courts....

The present case involves all of the elements that have made the Guarantee Clause cases non-justiciable. It is, in effect, a Guarantee Clause claim masquerading under a different label. But it cannot make the case more fit for judicial action that appellants invoke the Fourteenth Amendment rather than Art. IV, §4, where, in fact, the gist of their complaint is the same—unless it can be found that the Fourteenth Amendment speaks with greater particularity to their situation. We have been admonished to avoid "the tyranny of labels."...

But appellants, of course, do not rest on this claim simpliciter. In invoking the Equal Protection Clause, they assert that the distortion of representative government complained of is produced by systematic discrimination against them, by way of "a debasement of their votes...." Does this characterization, with due regard for the facts from which it is derived, add anything to appellants' case?

At first blush, this charge of discrimination based on legislative underrepresentation is given the appearance of a more private, less impersonal claim, than the assertion that the frame of government is askew. Appellants appear as representatives of a class that is prejudiced as a class, in contradistinction to the polity in its entirety. However, the discrimination relied on is the deprivation of what appellants conceive to be their proportionate share of political influence. This, of course, is the practical effect of any allocation of power within the institutions of government. Hardly any distribution of political authority that could be assailed as rendering government non-republican would fail similarly to operate to the prejudice of some groups, and to the advantage of others, within the body politic. It would be ingenuous not to see, or consciously blind to deny, that the real battle over the initiative and referendum, or over a delegation of power to local rather than state-wide authority, is the battle between forces whose influence is disparate among the various organs of government to whom power may be given. No shift of power but works a corresponding shift in political influence among the groups composing a society.

What, then, is this question of legislative apportionment? Appellants invoke the right to vote and to have their votes counted. But they are permitted to vote and their votes are counted. They go to the polls, they cast their ballots, they send their representatives to the state councils. Their complaint is simply that the representatives are not sufficiently numerous or powerful—in short, that Tennessee has adopted a basis of representation with which they are dissatisfied. Talk of "debasement" or "dilution" is circular talk. One cannot speak of "debasement" or "dilution" of the value of a vote until there is first defined a standard of reference as to what a vote should be worth. What is actually asked of the Court in this case is to choose among competing bases of representation—ultimately, really, among competing theories of political philosophy—in order to establish an appropriate frame of government for the State of Tennessee and thereby for all the States of the Union. . . .

To find such a political conception legally enforceable in the broad and unspecific guarantee of equal protection is to rewrite the Constitution. Certainly, "equal protection" is no more secure a foundation for judicial judgment of the permissibility of varying forms of representative government than is "Republican Form." Indeed since "equal protection of the laws" can only mean an equality of persons standing in the same relation to whatever governmental action is challenged, the determination whether treatment is equal presupposes a determination concerning the nature of the relationship. This, with respect to apportionment, means an inquiry into the theoretic base of representation in an acceptably republican state. For a court could not determine the equal protection issue without in fact first determining the Republican-Form issue, simply because what is reasonable for equal-protection purposes will depend upon what frame of government, basically, is allowed. To divorce "equal protection" from "Republican Form" is to talk about half a question.

The notion that representation proportioned to the geographic spread of population is so universally accepted as a necessary element of equality between man and man that it must be taken to be the standard of a political equality preserved by the Fourteenth Amendment—that it is, in appellants' words "the basic principle of representative government"—is, to put it bluntly, not true. However desirable and however desired by

some among the great political thinkers and framers of our
government, it has never been generally practiced, today or in
the past. It was not the English system, it was not the colonial
system, it was not the system chosen for the national government by the Constitution, it was not the system exclusively or
even predominantly practiced by the States at the time of adoption of the Fourteenth Amendment, it is not predominantly
practiced by the States today. Unless judges, the judges of this
Court, are to make their private views of political wisdom the
measure of the Constitution—views which in all honesty cannot but give the appearance, if not reflect the reality, of involvement with the business of partisan politics so inescapably a part
of apportionment controversies—the Fourteenth Amendment,
"itself a historical product," provides no guide for judicial oversight of the representation problem. . . .

Manifestly, the Equal Protection Clause supplies no clearer
guide for judicial examination of apportionment methods than
would the Guarantee Clause itself. Apportionment, by its character, is a subject of extraordinary complexity, involving—even
after the fundamental theoretical issues concerning what is to
be represented in a representative legislature have been fought
out or compromised—considerations of geography, demogra-
phy, electoral convenience, economic and social cohesions or
divergencies among particular local groups, communications,
the practical effects of political institutions like the lobby and
the city machine, ancient traditions and ties of settled usage,
respect for proven incumbents of long experience and senior
status, mathematical mechanics, censuses compiling relevant
data, and a host of others. Legislative responses throughout the
country to the reapportionment demands of the 1960 Census
have glaringly confirmed that these are not factors that lend
themselves to evaluations of a nature that are the staple of judi-

cial determinations or for which judges are equipped to adjudicate by legal training or experience or native wit. And this is the more so true because in every strand of this complicated, intricate web of values meet the contending forces of partisan politics. The practical significance of apportionment is that the next election results may differ because of it. Apportionment battles are overwhelmingly party or intra-party contests. It will add a virulent source of friction and tension in federal-state relations to embroil the federal judiciary in them....

Dissenting opinion of MR. JUSTICE HARLAN, whom MR. JUSTICE FRANKFURTER joins....

In the last analysis, what lies at the core of this controversy is a difference of opinion as to the function of representative government. It is surely beyond argument that those who have the responsibility for devising a system of representation may permissibly consider that factors other than bare numbers should be taken into account. The existence of the United States Senate is proof enough of that. To consider that we may ignore the Tennessee Legislature's judgment in this instance because that body was the product of an asymmetrical electoral apportionment would in effect be to assume the very conclusion here disputed. Hence we must accept the present form of the Tennessee Legislature as the embodiment of the State's choice, or, more realistically, its compromise, between competing political philosophies. The federal courts have not been empowered by the Equal Protection Clause to judge whether this resolution of the State's internal political conflict is desirable or undesirable, wise or unwise....

In short, there is nothing in the Federal Constitution to prevent a State, acting not irrationally, from choosing any electoral legislative structure it thinks best suited to the interests, temper, and customs of its people. . . . A State's choice to distribute electoral strength among geographical units, rather than according to a census of population, is certainly no less a rational decision of policy than would be its choice to levy a tax on property rather than a tax on income. Both are legislative judgments entitled to equal respect from this Court. . . .

From a reading of the majority and concurring opinions one will not find it difficult to catch the premises that underlie this decision. The fact that the appellants have been unable to obtain political redress of their asserted grievances appears to be regarded as a matter which should lead the Court to stretch to find some basis for judicial intervention. While the Equal Protection Clause is invoked, the opinion for the Court notably eschews explaining how, consonant with past decisions, the undisputed facts in this case can be considered to show a violation of that constitutional provision. The majority seems to have accepted the argument, pressed at the bar, that if this Court merely asserts authority in this field, Tennessee and other "malapportioning" States will quickly respond with appropriate political action, so that this Court need not be greatly concerned about the federal courts becoming further involved in these matters. At the same time the majority has wholly failed to reckon with what the future may hold in store if this optimistic prediction is not fulfilled. Thus, what the Court is doing reflects more an adventure in judicial experimentation than a solid piece of constitutional adjudication. . . .

In conclusion, it is appropriate to say that one need not agree, as a citizen, with what Tennessee has done or failed to do, in order to deprecate, as a judge, what the majority is doing today. Those observers of the Court who see it primarily as the last refuge for the correction of all inequality or injustice, no matter what its nature or source, will no doubt applaud this decision and its break with the past. Those who consider that continuing national respect for the Court's authority depends in large measure upon its wise exercise of self-restraint and discipline in constitutional adjudication, will view the decision with deep concern.

⚜   ⚜   ⚜

Justices Frankfurter and Harlan were wildly wrong about one thing, and fundamentally right about another. Both stressed the risks the Court was taking by intervening in the question of legislative apportionment. They feared that legislators would strike back at the Court. And indeed, for a brief period the risk of retaliation—by taking the power to order reapportionment away from the courts—seemed likely. Once reapportionment came, though, the Court's decisions became enormously popular. And understandably so: many people who had been frustrated by their inability to get malapportioned local legislatures to respond to their concerns now found themselves with new political power. Although the impetus behind reapportionment litigation came from underrepresented urban areas, as in Tennessee, it soon became clear that the real beneficiaries were the large numbers of people who had come to live in the nation's expanding suburbs. Rural interests suffered, of course, but the suburbs flourished with their new power in state legislatures. Rather than weakening the Court's reputation, the reapportionment decisions strengthened it.

At first, so did the underlying vision of politics that animated the decisions. Chief Justice Earl Warren called *Baker v. Carr* and the ensuing decisions the most notable legacy of his Court, the decisions that captured the essence of the Warren Court's vision of democracy. The phrase, "One person, one vote," was easy to understand and hard to quarrel with. Chief

Justice Warren's statement in a follow-up case, that "legislators represent people, not trees or acres," also expressed an important and widely held view about what politics was about.

As time went on, though, the weaknesses of the Court's approach became more apparent. The Court rapidly adopted rather rigid rules requiring that legislative districts have populations as close as feasible to each other. The Court's reasons were good ones—anything else would either have returned to the pre-*Baker* situation where virtually any apportionment would be constitutional, or have been impossible for the courts to administer fairly. But requiring strict mathematical equality pushed apportionment decisions toward serious *political* gerrymandering. Particularly as computerized methods of drawing district lines became widespread in the 1990s, partisan gerrymandering took root—and the Court, again for good reasons, refrained from limiting its use. Partisan gerrymandering, in turn, weakened American democracy, despite *Baker v. Carr's* hope that fairer apportionment would strengthen it. Partisan gerrymandering made it increasingly difficult to defeat incumbents in gerrymandered districts, and left adherents to the minority party in those districts truly disempowered.

Was there a way to avoid these results? Almost certainly not by staying out of the field entirely, as Justice Frankfurter urged. His hope that politics would remedy malapportionment seems especially unrealistic: it is hard to imagine the political circumstances under which politicians who held power because of malapportionment would draw district lines that would take their jobs away from them. Justice Harlan's dissent hints at one possibility: perhaps the Court could have insisted that legislative apportionments be defensible under *some* articulated theory of political representation. It is not crazy to think, for example, that legislators who represent people also ought to worry about the environment in rural areas—ought to represent trees and acres, in Chief Justice Warren's words. Giving representatives from rural areas somewhat more political power than they would get under a rule of strict population equality might make sense as a matter of political theory.

One way to develop such an approach would have been to use traditional notions of equal protection, as the Court in *Baker* asserted. Still, Justice Frankfurter's disparagement of that "soothing" assertion has some bite: once you let legislatures build apportionments around "reasonable" theories of political representation, you are going to open up the field to almost anything—not much of an improvement on the situation before *Baker*.

The dissent in *Baker v. Carr* argued that the decision, because it was wrong, would be unpopular. Making that connection was a mistake. *Baker* may be wrong, but it was enormously popular, to the point that it is almost entirely uncontroversial today. What we may need, and what the dissents do not provide us, is some way to talk about wrong but popular decisions. The Introduction suggested that great dissents like that in *Plessy v. Ferguson* are vindicated by history, which means that they reject decisions that are popular at the time but that become unpopular. What, though, of decisions like the reapportionment cases that have not (yet) become unpopular? Justice Frankfurter's dissent seems somewhat cranky, but that way of reading it may be inevitable as long as the majority opinion remains popular.

We might think about our reactions to dissents in cases that remain important and controversial today: What do supporters of abortion rights think of dissents from decisions striking down restrictive laws? And what do opponents of affirmative action and integration think of dissents from decisions limiting those programs?

CHAPTER 13

"A sterile metaphor which by its very nature may distort rather than illumine the problems."

Abington School District v. Schempp, 1963

In 1963 no one on the Supreme Court thought that holding it unconstitutional to open the day at public schools with readings from the Bible would be terribly controversial. A year earlier the Court had struck down what everyone thought was a quite similar practice in New York, where teachers read the state-drafted nondenominational prayer at the beginning of the day. There was some public outcry, and a number of constitutional amendments were proposed to overturn the Court's ruling. But, at least from inside the Court, the rhetoric seemed to outrun the reality of public concern. Nor did anyone—on the Court or elsewhere—seem troubled in the early 1960s by well settled law making it clear that any student who objected to participating in the prayer activity had to be excused from doing so.

Even more, secularization seemed to have advanced significantly in the decades after World War II. Politicians paid lip service to the "Judaeo-Christian tradition," but no public figure appeared to make faith a central part of his life. President Dwight Eisenhower captured this diffuse religiosity in his purported statement, "America makes no sense unless it is founded in a deeply felt religious faith—and I don't care what it is."

Of course the Court could have treated generic school

prayers as an example of precisely that sort of diffuse religiosity. The justices were more secular than the rest of the society, though, and they viewed school prayers as a minor benefit to the religious and a major insult to secularists.

Ellory Schempp was a slightly rebellious teenager from a Unitarian Universalist family in suburban Philadelphia when he began to protest a state law requiring that ten Bible verses be read at the start of each school day by bringing a Koran to class and reading from it. (He has since become a distinguished physicist who worked on the development of MRI—magnetic resonance imaging—techniques.) A similar challenge in Maryland was mounted by Madalyn Murray, who later became perhaps the nation's most famous atheist activist. The Schempps and the Murrays urged the Court to hold that reciting prayers at the beginning of the school day amounted to establishing religion in violation of the First Amendment's non-establishment clause. Applying that provision to state laws was a bit tricky. The clause reads, "Congress shall make no law respecting an establishment of religion." It is reasonably clear that the clause was aimed at preventing Congress from establishing a national religion and from interfering with whatever system of church-state relations individual states chose to have. It was within acceptable bounds to argue that some leading figures in the founding generation would have regarded school prayers as an establishment of religion, although probably only a few. But the First Amendment, as adopted in 1791, would have let states have such establishments if they wanted them.

In the 1930s and 1940s the Supreme Court began "incorporating" the Bill of Rights into the Fourteenth Amendment. The doctrinal path was complex and messy. Partly the explanation the Court offered was that those who adopted the Fourteenth Amendment wanted to apply the Bill of Rights to the states.

How could the non-establishment clause be applied to the states, though? By holding that if a practice would be an establishment of religion if Congress ordered it, the Fourteenth Amendment barred the states from adopting the same practice. The Court took that step in 1947. Further, the Court hinted that what mattered was not whether a practice would have been regarded as an establishment of religion in 1791, but rather whether it would have been so regarded in 1868 when the Fourteenth Amendment was adopted.

Justice Tom Clark's majority opinion was straightforward and workmanlike. It marched through the precedents, and concluded that the non-establishment principle was designed to promote a healthy "neutrality" on the government's part with respect to religion. Reading from the Bible at the start of the school day was obviously a religious activity, and requiring such reading violated the non-establishment clause. The decision's major contribution to constitutional doctrine was its formulation of a standard for determining when the establishment clause is violated: statutes had to have "a secular legislative purpose and a primary effect that neither advances nor inhibits religion." That standard has endured, though subsequent experience showed that applying it to the variety of non-establishment problems that the courts began to confront was not an easy task.

Lurking in the case was another issue. The Schempps and Murrays presented psychological evidence in the lower courts supporting their claim that students felt pressure from the schools and from their classmates to participate in the prayers rather than leave the classroom during them, as the schools allowed. Forcing someone to participate in a prayer would certainly violate the Constitution's protection of the "free exercise" of religion. Justice Potter Stewart's dissent focuses on this possibility, although he thought that the cases did not have enough evidence about coercion to allow him to make a final judgment on the free exercise issue.

⚜   ⚜   ⚜

Mr. Justice Stewart, dissenting.

I think the records in the two cases before us are so fundamentally deficient as to make impossible an informed or responsible determination of the constitutional issues presented. Specifically, I cannot agree that on these records we can say that the Establishment Clause has necessarily been violated. But I think there exist serious questions under both that provision and the Free Exercise Clause—insofar as each is imbedded in the Fourteenth Amendment—which require the remand of these cases for the taking of additional evidence.

The First Amendment declares that "Congress shall make no law respecting an establishment of religion, or prohibiting the free exercise thereof...." It is, I think, a fallacious oversimplification to regard these two provisions as establishing a single constitutional standard of "separation of church and state," which can be mechanically applied in every case to delineate the required boundaries between government and religion. We err in the first place if we do not recognize, as a matter of history and as a matter of the imperatives of our free society, that religion and government must necessarily interact in countless ways. Secondly, the fact is that while in many contexts the Establishment Clause and the Free Exercise Clause fully complement each other, there are areas in which a doctrinaire reading of the Establishment Clause leads to irreconcilable conflict with the Free Exercise Clause.

A single obvious example should suffice to make the point. Spending federal funds to employ chaplains for the armed forces might be said to violate the Establishment Clause. Yet a lonely soldier stationed at some faraway outpost could surely complain that a government which did *not* provide him the opportunity for pastoral guidance was affirmatively prohibiting the free exercise of his religion. And such examples could readily be multiplied. The short of the matter is simply that the two relevant clauses of the First Amendment cannot accurately be reflected in a sterile metaphor which by its very nature may distort rather than illumine the problems involved in a particular case. . . .

As a matter of history, the First Amendment was adopted solely as a limitation upon the newly created National Government. The events leading to its adoption strongly suggest that the Establishment Clause was primarily an attempt to insure that Congress not only would be powerless to establish a national church, but would also be unable to interfere with existing state establishments. Each State was left free to go its own way and pursue its own policy with respect to religion. Thus Virginia from the beginning pursued a policy of disestablishmentarianism. Massachusetts, by contrast, had an established church until well into the nineteenth century.

So matters stood until the adoption of the Fourteenth Amendment, or more accurately, until this Court's decision in *Cantwell v. Connecticut*, in 1940. In that case the Court said: "The First Amendment declares that Congress shall make no law respecting an establishment of religion or prohibiting the free exercise thereof. The Fourteenth Amendment has rendered the legislatures of the states as incompetent as Congress to enact such laws." . . .

That the central value embodied in the First Amendment— and, more particularly, in the guarantee of "liberty" contained in the Fourteenth—is the safeguarding of an individual's right to free exercise of his religion has been consistently recognized.

Thus, in the case of *Hamilton v. Regents* [1934], Mr. Justice Cardozo, concurring, assumed that it was "... *the religious liberty* protected by the First Amendment against invasion by the nation [which] is protected by the Fourteenth Amendment against invasion by the states." (emphasis added) And in *Cantwell v. Connecticut*, the purpose of those guarantees was described in the following terms: "On the one hand, it forestalls compulsion by law of the acceptance of any creed or the practice of any form of worship. Freedom of conscience and freedom to adhere to such religious organization or form of worship as the individual may choose cannot be restricted by law. On the other hand, it safeguards the free exercise of the chosen form of religion."

It is this concept of constitutional protection embodied in our decisions which makes the cases before us such difficult ones for me. For there is involved in these cases a substantial free exercise claim on the part of those who affirmatively desire to have their children's school day open with the reading of passages from the Bible. . . .

It might also be argued that parents who want their children exposed to religious influences can adequately fulfill that wish off school property and outside school time. With all its surface persuasiveness, however, this argument seriously misconceives the basic constitutional justification for permitting the exercises at issue in these cases. For a compulsory state educational system so structures a child's life that if religious exercises are held to be an impermissible activity in schools, religion is placed at an artificial and state-created disadvantage. Viewed in this light, permission of such exercises for those who want them is necessary if the schools are truly to be neutral in the matter of religion. And a refusal to permit religious exercises thus is seen, not as the realization of state neutrality, but rather as the establishment of a religion of secularism, or at the least, as government support of the beliefs of those who think that religious exercises should be conducted only in private.

What seems to me to be of paramount importance, then, is recognition of the fact that the claim advanced here in favor of Bible reading is sufficiently substantial to make simple reference to the constitutional phrase "establishment of religion" as inadequate an analysis of the cases before us as the ritualistic invocation of the nonconstitutional phrase "separation of church and state." What these cases compel, rather, is an analysis of just what the "neutrality" is which is required by the interplay of the Establishment and Free Exercise Clauses of the First Amendment, as imbedded in the Fourteenth. . . .

I have said that these provisions authorizing religious exercises are properly to be regarded as measures making possible the free exercise of religion. But it is important to stress that, strictly speaking, what is at issue here is a privilege rather than a right. In other words, the question presented is not whether exercises such as those at issue here are constitutionally compelled, but rather whether they are constitutionally invalid. And that issue, in my view, turns on the question of coercion.

It is clear that the dangers of coercion involved in the holding of religious exercises in a schoolroom differ qualitatively from those presented by the use of similar exercises or affirmations in ceremonies attended by adults. Even as to children, however, the duty laid upon government in connection with religious exercises in the public schools is that of refraining from so structuring the school environment as to put any kind of pressure on a child to participate in those exercises; it is not that of providing an atmosphere in which children are kept scrupulously insulated from any awareness that some of their fellows may want to open the school day with prayer, or of the fact that there exist in our pluralistic society differences of religious belief. . . .

The governmental neutrality which the First and Fourteenth Amendments require in the cases before us, in other words, is the extension of evenhanded treatment to all who believe, doubt, or disbelieve—a refusal on the part of the State to weight the scales of private choice. In these cases, therefore, what is involved is not state action based on impermissible categories, but rather an attempt by the State to accommodate those differences which the existence in our society of a variety of religious beliefs makes inevitable. The Constitution requires that such efforts be struck down only if they are proven to entail the use of the secular authority of government to coerce a preference among such beliefs.

It may well be, as has been argued to us, that even the supposed benefits to be derived from noncoercive religious exercises in public schools are incommensurate with the administrative problems which they would create. The choice involved, however, is one for each local community and its school board, and not for this Court. For, as I have said, religious exercises are not constitutionally invalid if they simply reflect differences which exist in the society from which the school draws its pupils. They become constitutionally invalid only if their administration places the sanction of secular authority behind one or more particular religious or irreligious beliefs.

To be specific, it seems to me clear that certain types of exercises would present situations in which no possibility of coercion on the part of secular officials could be claimed to exist. Thus, if such exercises were held either before or after the official school day, or if the school schedule were such that participation were merely one among a number of desirable alternatives, it could hardly be contended that the exercises did anything more than to provide an opportunity for the voluntary expression of religious belief. On the other hand, a law which provided for religious exercises during the school day and which contained no excusal provision would obviously be unconstitutionally coercive upon those who did not wish to participate. And even under a law containing an excusal provision, if the exercises were held during the school day, and no equally desirable alternative were provided by the school authorities, the likelihood that children might be under at least some psychological compulsion to participate would be great. In a case such as the latter, however, I think we would err if we *assumed* such coercion in the absence of any evidence.

What our Constitution indispensably protects is the freedom of each of us, be he Jew or Agnostic, Christian or Atheist, Buddhist or Freethinker, to believe or disbelieve, to worship or not worship, to pray or keep silent, according to his own conscience, uncoerced and unrestrained by government. It is conceivable that these school boards, or even all school boards, might eventually find it impossible to administer a system of religious exercises during school hours in such a way as to meet this constitutional standard—in such a way as completely to free from any kind of official coercion those who do not affirmatively want to participate. But I think we must not assume that school boards so lack the qualities of inventiveness and good will as to make impossible the achievement of that goal....

⚜   ⚜   ⚜

The Court's school prayer decisions were quite controversial. For many years the practices the Court held unconstitutional persisted in many school districts. Even today there are recurrent reports of schools, mostly in small rural districts, where prayers continue to open the school day. By 2007, though, compliance with the Court's decisions appeared to be rather high.

What had happened was that prayer practices migrated—

from compulsory practices at the beginning of the school day to prayers at graduation ceremonies, or at football games. The Court found such practices unconstitutional too, but it is clear that "evasions"—or efforts by school systems to figure out ways in which prayers could be said within the constitutional framework the Court established—continued. Schools chose speakers from the graduating class according to criteria having nothing to do with religion—the class valedictorian, for example—and allowed the speaker to give a religiously infused talk. Football coaches, or student football captains, led their teams in prayers on the field before the kickoff.

The most important response to the Court's school prayer decision was not an evasion at all. Parents removed their children from public schools and sent them to newly organized private schools where religion was a central part of the curriculum. In the South these religious academies in their early years also allowed parents to avoid racially integrated schools, although eventually the racial distinctiveness of the religious academies weakened. Even more broadly, parents disaffected by the Court's prayer decisions became an important part of the so-called Christian Right as a conservative political movement.

Would these consequences have occurred if Justice Stewart's dissent had prevailed? Probably so—because Justice Stewart's approach *might* have placed many school prayer practices under a constitutional cloud, and because too many other forces fueled the rise of the Christian Right. In form, the practices the Court found unconstitutional were voluntary: students who did not want to say the prayers did not have to do so. But Justice Stewart thought that sometimes prayer practices would in effect be compulsory. How often? We do not know, because the Court did not follow Justice Stewart's approach. What we do know is that as the Court's jurisprudence about public prayers developed, a majority of the justices did come to focus on the possibility of coercion—and found coercion in, for example, a prayer said at a graduation ceremony (*Lee v. Weisman*, 1992). If graduating high school students were coerced when a rabbi or minister said a prayer at the ceremony, certainly elementary school students would be coerced by ordinary prayers said at the opening of each school day.

Some parts of the Christian Right's concerns dealt with Supreme Court decisions and their consequences: the school prayer decisions, but also desegregation and eventually the Court's abortion decisions. But much more went into the rise of the Christian Right than constitutional law. The social turmoil of the 1960s and the upsurge in commitments among many Americans to strong versions of an ideology of personal autonomy—associated with ideas of sexual liberation and feminism generated a sense among members of the Christian Right that the nation had taken a wrong turn. The Court's decisions might have provided a focal point for some of the Christian Right's rhetoric, but that rhetoric would have attached itself to something else had the Court never addressed the issues of concern to the Christian Right.

But, of course, the Court almost inevitably did address such issues, because there were *other* social movements in the field—the movements that the Court's decisions endorsed. And, as we will see in Chapter 16, whatever the Court did—rule against school prayer or uphold it—would have been understood by one side or the other as endorsing their views and rejecting their opponents'. The Court could not avoid taking sides and thereby giving contending political movements some rhetorical hooks for their concerns.

Finally, the observation that the Court eventually found coercion in perhaps surprising places raises deep questions about projecting the effects of the imagined adoption by the Court of a view expressed by a dissenter. Are we to imagine the very same judges who found school prayers unconstitutional asking whether Bible reading and prayer actually coerced high school students? If so, we can be reasonably sure what answer they would give. And yet, if we imagine an entirely different set of judges asking that question, the range of answers expands enormously. A different group of justices, for example, might conclude from Justice Stewart's analysis of parents' Free Exercise interests that school prayers might be *required* by the Constitution, not merely permitted by it. And beyond that, the horizon seems quite unbounded.

CHAPTER 14

"I get nowhere in this case by talk about a constitutional 'right of privacy.'"

Griswold v. Connecticut, 1965

Earl Warren's Supreme Court took part in a "rights revolution." From Warren's appointment in 1954 through 1962, the Court was clearly leaning to the left but, except for its decision in *Brown v. Board of Education,* was relatively cautious. That changed in 1962, when Justice Frankfurter retired because of ill health. From then until Warren's retirement in 1973 the Court was decidedly liberal. At its heart the Warren Court's rights revolution dealt with equality and political participation. The school desegregation cases (Chapter 11) were only one part of the Warren Court's effort to address racial discrimination. Many of the Warren Court's criminal procedure decisions extending the reach of the Constitution into police stations and local jails directly raised questions about racial justice, and the Court's interventions were almost certainly motivated by a general concern that criminal justice was being administered in a racially biased way. The Court's voting rights decisions (Chapter 12) were obviously about equality, and sometimes about racial equality as well. But the voting rights cases were also about making sure that the American political process operated in a fair and democratic manner. The Warren Court's expansive interpretations of the Constitution's guarantee of free expression had the same goal.

179

No matter how controversial each decision was, each fit comfortably within the tradition of American political liberalism. The Warren Court collaborated with the nation's Congress and the presidency as shaped by the New Deal, John F. Kennedy's New Frontier, and Lyndon B. Johnson's Great Society visions. In the 1960s liberalism changed or—in the view of some—deepened. Concern for democracy and equality was supplemented by an interest in promoting individual autonomy, which to some theorists provided the best explanation of the constitutional rights to equality and democratic participation anyway. This development in constitutional theory paralleled social change as well, with the rise of a "do your own thing" ideology more broadly.

In light of these developments, it is hardly surprising that constitutional law began to pay attention to personal autonomy, or that its attention first focused on sex (and not drugs—or rock-and-roll). On standard accounts the sexual revolution of the 1960s rested on the availability of safe contraceptives, and specifically on the development and ready availability of contraceptive drugs. There were some holdouts against the sexual revolution, though. Out of a combination of principle and legislative inertia, a handful of states retained laws on their books that made it difficult for people to obtain contraceptives.

Connecticut was one of those states. It had what was probably the most stringent anticontraceptive law on the nation's books, making it a crime to use contraceptives. No one was ever prosecuted for doing so, of course, but with using contraceptives a crime, other parts of the state's criminal code kicked in. Doctors, pharmacies, and—importantly—family planning clinics could be prosecuted for aiding and abetting the use of contraceptives by distributing birth control pills. Prosecutors would not go after husbands and wives who used contraceptives, but they had no hesitation in prosecuting family planning clinics—or at least in threatening to prosecute them, which was enough to keep the clinics from operating as effectively as they would like.

From the 1940s on leaders in Connecticut's family planning movement, including actress Katharine Hepburn's mother, tried to get the state's laws modified or abolished. They lobbied the state's legislature, but the state's Catholic lawmakers blocked repeal. They filed lawsuits, but each one failed because no one had been prosecuted for violating the state's laws. Finally, in 1961 they decided to invite prosecution by opening a family planning clinic in New Haven, where they would openly violate the state's anticontraceptive law. The local prosecutor did the expected and prosecuted the clinic's director and chief medical official for aiding and abetting the use of contraceptives.

The Supreme Court reversed their convictions, handing a major victory to those fighting for this right to privacy. Writing for the Court, Justice William O. Douglas, a veteran of the New Deal's battle against the conservative Court of the 1930s (Chapter 8), disclaimed any intention to return to the discredited era when the Court relied on the due process clause to strike down state laws (Chapter 6). In an opinion whose merits scholars continue to debate, Justice Douglas purported to rely on explicit constitutional texts. "Various guarantees create zones of privacy," he wrote, citing the First, Third, Fourth, and Fifth amendments. Referring to earlier decisions striking down statutes that did not obviously conflict with the Constitution's specific terms, he observed that the cases "suggest that specific guarantees in the Bill of Rights have penumbras, formed by emanations from those guarantees that help give them life and substance." He concluded, "We deal with a right of privacy older than the Bill of Rights."

Justice Arthur Goldberg added in a separate opinion joined

by two others that the right to privacy might also be founded in the Ninth Amendment, which says, "The enumeration, in the Constitution, of certain rights, shall not be construed to deny or disparage others retained by the people." According to Justice Goldberg, this provision assumed that the people *had* rights that were not specifically spelled out in the Constitution, and for the courts to refuse to enforce such unenumerated rights just as they enforced enumerated ones would "disparage" them.

Justice Hugo Black dissented, as did Justice Potter Stewart. As senator from Alabama, Justice Black had been a strong supporter of the New Deal and the Court-packing plan (Chapter 8). He was rewarded—and the New Deal's opponents given the back of Roosevelt's hand—with Roosevelt's first Supreme Court appointment in 1937. Famous for carrying a copy of the Constitution in his pocket wherever he went, Justice Black said that he read the Constitution's words literally. When the First Amendment said "Congress shall make no law . . . abridging the freedom of speech," Justice Black said it meant "no law" whatever. This literalism gave Justice Black's opinions an appealing simplicity, but simplicity had the downside of sometimes forcing Justice Black into doctrinal contortions, for example, over whether something that actually communicated a message— like a picket line—was "speech" or "action." Justice Black's dissent in *Griswold* exemplifies one aspect of his literalist approach to constitutional interpretation.

⚜   ⚜   ⚜

Mr. Justice Black, with whom Mr. Justice Stewart joins, dissenting.

I agree with my Brother Stewart's dissenting opinion. And like him I do not to any extent whatever base my view that this

Connecticut law is constitutional on a belief that the law is wise or that its policy is a good one. In order that there may be no room at all to doubt why I vote as I do, I feel constrained to add that the law is every bit as offensive to me as it is to my Brethren of the majority and my Brothers Harlan, White and Goldberg who, reciting reasons why it is offensive to them, hold it unconstitutional. There is no single one of the graphic and eloquent strictures and criticisms fired at the policy of this Connecticut law either by the Court's opinion or by those of my concurring Brethren to which I cannot subscribe—except their conclusion that the evil qualities they see in the law make it unconstitutional. . . .

The Court talks about a constitutional "right of privacy" as though there is some constitutional provision or provisions forbidding any law ever to be passed which might abridge the "privacy" of individuals. But there is not. There are, of course, guarantees in certain specific constitutional provisions which are designed in part to protect privacy at certain times and places with respect to certain activities. Such, for example, is the Fourth Amendment's guarantee against "unreasonable searches and seizures." But I think it belittles that Amendment to talk about it as though it protects nothing but "privacy." To treat it that way is to give it a niggardly interpretation, not the kind of liberal reading I think any Bill of Rights provision should be given. The average man would very likely not have his feelings soothed any more by having his property seized openly than by having it seized privately and by stealth. He simply wants his property left alone. And a person can be just as much, if not more, irritated, annoyed and injured by an unceremonious public arrest by a policeman as he is by a seizure in the privacy of his office or home.

One of the most effective ways of diluting or expanding a constitutionally guaranteed right is to substitute for the crucial

word or words of a constitutional guarantee another word or
words, more or less flexible and more or less restricted in meaning. This fact is well illustrated by the use of the term "right of
privacy" as a comprehensive substitute for the Fourth Amendment's guarantee against "unreasonable searches and seizures."
"Privacy" is a broad, abstract and ambiguous concept which
can easily be shrunken in meaning but which can also, on the
other hand, easily be interpreted as a constitutional ban against
many things other than searches and seizures. I have expressed
the view many times that First Amendment freedoms, for example, have suffered from a failure of the courts to stick to the
simple language of the First Amendment in construing it, instead of invoking multitudes of words substituted for those the
Framers used. For these reasons I get nowhere in this case by
talk about a constitutional "right of privacy" as an emanation
from one or more constitutional provisions. I like my privacy as
well as the next one, but I am nevertheless compelled to admit
that government has a right to invade it unless prohibited by
some specific constitutional provision. For these reasons I cannot agree with the Court's judgment and the reasons it gives for
holding this Connecticut law unconstitutional. . . .

My Brother Goldberg has adopted the recent discovery that
the Ninth Amendment as well as the Due Process Clause can be
used by this Court as authority to strike down all state legislation which this Court thinks violates "fundamental principles
of liberty and justice," or is contrary to the "traditions and [col-
lective] conscience of our people." He also states, without proof
satisfactory to me, that in making decisions on this basis judges
will not consider "their personal and private notions." One may
ask how they can avoid considering them. Our Court certainly
has no machinery with which to take a Gallup Poll. And the
8scientific miracles of this age have not yet produced a gadget

which the Court can use to determine what traditions are rooted in the "[collective] conscience of our people." Moreover, one would certainly have to look far beyond the language of the Ninth Amendment to find that the Framers vested in this Court any such awesome veto powers over lawmaking, either by the States or by the Congress. Nor does anything in the history of the Amendment offer any support for such a shocking doctrine. The whole history of the adoption of the Constitution and Bill of Rights points the other way, and the very material quoted by my Brother Goldberg shows that the Ninth Amendment was intended to protect against the idea that "by enumerating particular exceptions to the grant of power" to the Federal Government, "those rights which were not singled out, were intended to be assigned into the hands of the General Government [the United States], and were consequently insecure." That Amendment was passed, not to broaden the powers of this Court or any other department of "the General Government," but, as every student of history knows, to assure the people that the Constitution in all its provisions was intended to limit the Federal Government to the powers granted expressly or by necessary implication. If any broad, unlimited power to hold laws unconstitutional because they offend what this Court conceives to be the "[collective] conscience of our people" is vested in this Court by the Ninth Amendment, the Fourteenth Amendment, or any other provision of the Constitution, it was not given by the Framers, but rather has been bestowed on the Court by the Court. This fact is perhaps responsible for the peculiar phenomenon that for a period of a century and a half no serious suggestion was ever made that the Ninth Amendment, enacted to protect state powers against federal invasion, could be used as a weapon of federal power to prevent state legislatures from passing laws they consider ap-

propriate to govern local affairs. Use of any such broad, unbounded judicial authority would make of this Court's members a day-to-day constitutional convention. . . .

I repeat so as not to be misunderstood that this Court does
have power, which it should exercise, to hold laws unconstitutional where they are forbidden by the Federal Constitution.
My point is that there is no provision of the Constitution
which either expressly or impliedly vests power in this Court to
sit as a supervisory agency over acts of duly constituted legislative bodies and set aside their laws because of the Court's belief
that the legislative policies adopted are unreasonable, unwise,
arbitrary, capricious or irrational. The adoption of such a loose,
flexible, uncontrolled standard for holding laws unconstitutional, if ever it is finally achieved, will amount to a great unconstitutional shift of power to the courts which I believe and
am constrained to say will be bad for the courts and worse for
the country. Subjecting federal and state laws to such an unrestrained and unrestrainable judicial control as to the wisdom of
legislative enactments would, I fear, jeopardize the separation
of governmental powers that the Framers set up and at the same
time threaten to take away much of the power of States to govern themselves which the Constitution plainly intended them
to have. . . .

MR. JUSTICE STEWART, whom MR. JUSTICE BLACK joins,
dissenting.

Since 1879 Connecticut has had on its books a law which
forbids the use of contraceptives by anyone. I think this is an
uncommonly silly law. As a practical matter, the law is obviously unenforceable, except in the oblique context of the
present case. As a philosophical matter, I believe the use of contraceptives in the relationship of marriage should be left to per-

sonal and private choice, based upon each individual's moral, ethical, and religious beliefs. As a matter of social policy, I think professional counsel about methods of birth control should be available to all, so that each individual's choice can be meaningfully made. But we are not asked in this case to say whether we think this law is unwise, or even asinine. We are asked to hold that it violates the United States Constitution. And that I cannot do....

At the oral argument in this case we were told that the Connecticut law does not "conform to current community standards." But it is not the function of this Court to decide cases on the basis of community standards. We are here to decide cases "agreeably to the Constitution and laws of the United States." It is the essence of judicial duty to subordinate our own personal views, our own ideas of what legislation is wise and what is not. If, as I should surely hope, the law before us does not reflect the standards of the people of Connecticut, the people of Connecticut can freely exercise their true Ninth and Tenth Amendment rights to persuade their elected representatives to repeal it. That is the constitutional way to take this law off the books.

✠ ✠ ✠

The dissenters would have left it to Connecticut's voters to deal with their "uncommonly silly" statute. The sexual revolution washing over the nation left the state's anticontraceptive law isolated. Many Connecticut residents—those who could readily drive into neighboring New York, for example—could already obtain contraceptives, and the statute's real effect was to keep family planning offices from openly distributing contraceptives. It is hard to believe that the statute could have survived for more than a few years longer.

Griswold struck down a law, described even by the dissenters as silly, that no other state had. Its immediate practical effects were unimportant, although family planning agencies did open their doors in Connecticut after the decision. Its more important effects were in creating or acknowledging a constitutional right of privacy, better described as a right of personal autonomy. *Griswold* provided the resources within constitutional doctrine for the far more controversial decision less than a decade later in *Roe v. Wade* to invalidate most of the nation's laws restricting the availability of abortion. *Griswold*'s right to privacy became a right to make personal choices about sexual intimacy and its consequences—which, after *Roe,* eventually became the predicate for the Court's gay rights decision invalidating antisodomy laws (see Chapter 16).

Would the dissenters' views in *Griswold* have forestalled these developments? Taken most broadly, those views cautioned strongly against resting constitutional decisions on rights not specifically set out in the Constitution—and no one thinks, even today, that a right of personal autonomy is explicitly listed in the Bill of Rights. Yet we must also understand two things. First, lawyers will always be available to come up with arguments that silly laws are unconstitutional, and people who think the laws are silly are going to tend to find those arguments convincing. Second, and more important, social changes —the sexual revolution, the transformation of women's lives in the late twentieth century—also change the way people think about the Constitution.

All the dissenters demanded was something in the Constitution on which to rest the Court's decision. They criticized the suggestion that the Ninth Amendment was enough. The Ninth Amendment's meaning is notoriously unclear. Judge Robert Bork suggested that the provision resembled a statement, "People shall have the right," with the rest of the sentence obscured by an inkblot. Still, there it is in the Constitution, saying that listing specific rights in the Constitution should not be taken as implying that people did not have *other* rights. A later Supreme Court blocked by the *Griswold* dissenters' general constitutional theory might have found the Ninth Amendment enough to satisfy the dissenters' demand for language in the Constitution as a predicate for invalidating restrictive abortion laws—and might have been motivated to do so by the social changes that propelled the decisions as they actually were.

Popular constitutionalism (see Chapter 2) offers an alternative. The dissenters' insisted on specific constitutional language because they worried about the justification for *judicial* action invalidating statutes. Popular constitutionalism operates outside the courts. In its most modest form, popular constitutionalism might have generated arguments that the anticontraceptive law—and restrictive abortion laws, and more—should be amended or repealed because they were inconsistent with a constitutional right to privacy or personal autonomy that the people themselves enforced. A more robust form of popular constitutionalism would let the courts see what the people had done *legislatively* and infer from that some propositions about what the people understood the Constitution to mean. In this version, the courts notice a movement across the nation and jump on the bandwagon, getting rid of statutes in states that have not quite caught up to the rest of the country. That, it could be said, is precisely what happened in *Griswold*.

Roe v. Wade shows the risk of this version of popular constitutionalism. The courts might jump on the wrong bandwagon, or might jump on just at the point where the bandwagon is about to come to a screeching halt. They *think* they are acting on behalf of the people's constitutional views, but they are mistaken. Law professor Alexander Bickel suggested that the Supreme Court worked best when it successfully predicted the future. Bickel's idea gains support as well from the idea that what makes a dissent great is that it is vindicated by history. Yet we might wonder how good judges are at that task—at least if they self-consciously appeal to the future in their opinions or dissents. Perhaps judges will do their job best if they think only about what the Constitution, as they understand it, means, rather than about what is happening in the society as a whole.

CHAPTER 15

"That is what this suit is about. Power."

Morrison v. Olson, 1988

The botched 1972 burglary of the Democratic party's offices at the Watergate office complex in Washington, D.C., and the ensuing efforts by high officials in the Nixon administration, including the president himself, to cover up official involvement in the episode, brought public attention to a persistent problem in designing democratic institutions: what do you do about high-level wrongdoing, especially when that wrongdoing is hidden from view? Once the public knows about the wrongdoing, political mechanisms like impeachment can kick in. But impeachment is something like a nuclear weapon—good to hold in reserve, not so good to use.

The response to the revelations about Watergate occurred in three stages. News accounts of the coverup placed so much pressure on the Nixon administration that in 1973 it appointed a special prosecutor, Archibald Cox, who was nominally—and, it turned out, actually—under the attorney general's control. Cox's investigation eventually led to the discovery of audio tapes of conversations between the president and his aides. Cox believed that hearing the tapes would advance his investigation. Nixon ordered Cox to withdraw his subpoenas for the tapes. When Cox refused, the president directed Attorney General Elliott Richardson to fire Cox. Believing that doing so would violate a pledge he had made to the Senate, Richardson refused to do so, and resigned, along with several of his assistants. The last person standing was Solicitor General Robert Bork, who did fire Cox in what came to be known as the Saturday Night Massacre.

The ensuing storm of protest forced Nixon to retreat. He had the attorney general appoint a new special prosecutor, Leon Jaworski, who eventually obtained the tapes after persuading the Supreme Court to uphold an order directing that the tapes be turned over to him. In August 1974 Nixon resigned in the face of near-certain impeachment.

Finally, believing that the process of investigating high-level wrongdoing was too cumbersome and entailed unnecessary national turmoil, Congress responded by enacting the Ethics in Government Act of 1978. Under that act, an Attorney General who received significant evidence of high-level wrongdoing was required to request the appointment of an independent counsel by a special three-judge court whose members were appointed by the Chief Justice. Once appointed, the independent counsel had much more latitude than an ordinary prosecutor, although there were some quite unusual circumstances under which an independent counsel could be dismissed by the president.

Supporters of presidential power, mostly Republicans, argued that the statute was unconstitutional because it transferred a core presidential power—control over criminal prosecution—to someone substantially free from presidential direction. The Supreme Court addressed the constitutional argument when an independent counsel was appointed to investigate allegations that while serving as an assistant attorney general in the Department of Justice, Theodore Olson had given misleading testimony to a congressional committee looking into the Reagan administration's enforcement of federal environmental laws. (No charges resulted from the investigation, and Olson went on to become a well-respected Washington lawyer, who represented George W. Bush in the Supreme Court cases that led to Bush's installation as president, and then served as solicitor general.)

By a vote of seven-to-one the Supreme Court upheld the statute's constitutionality in an opinion by Chief Justice William Rehnquist. (Justice Anthony Kennedy did not participate in the case.) Much of the chief justice's opinion was devoted to technical constitutional questions, such as whether an independent counsel was an "inferior officer." (If so, the Constitution allows appointment by the courts.) The opinion concluded that the statute did not violate general principles of separation of powers by giving either Congress or the courts powers that undermined the president's. The opinion made much of the fact that the statute did preserve some presidential power to remove an independent counsel "for cause."

JUSTICE SCALIA, dissenting.

It is the proud boast of our democracy that we have "a government of laws and not of men." Many Americans are familiar with that phrase; not many know its derivation. It comes from Part the First, Article XXX, of the Massachusetts Constitution of 1780, which reads in full as follows:

> In the government of this Commonwealth, the legislative department shall never exercise the executive and judicial powers, or either of them: The executive shall never exercise the legislative and judicial powers, or either of them: The judicial shall never exercise the legislative and executive powers, or either of them: to the end it may be a government of laws and not of men.

The Framers of the Federal Constitution similarly viewed the principle of separation of powers as the absolutely central guarantee of a just Government.... Without a secure structure of separated powers, our Bill of Rights would be worthless, as are the bills of rights of many nations of the world that have adopted, or even improved upon, the mere words of ours....

... [T]he Founders conspicuously and very consciously declined to sap the Executive's strength in the same way they had weakened the Legislature: by dividing the executive power. Proposals to have multiple executives, or a council of advisers with separate authority were rejected. Thus, while "[a]ll legislative Powers herein granted shall be vested in a Congress of the United States, which shall consist of a Senate and House of Representatives," "[t]he executive Power shall be vested in a President of the United States."

That is what this suit is about. Power. The allocation of power among Congress, the President, and the courts in such fashion as to preserve the equilibrium the Constitution sought to establish—so that "a gradual concentration of the several powers in the same department" can effectively be resisted. Frequently an issue of this sort will come before the Court clad, so to speak, in sheep's clothing: the potential of the asserted principle to effect important change in the equilibrium of power is not immediately evident, and must be discerned by a careful and perceptive analysis. But this wolf comes as a wolf....

Thus, by the application of this statute in the present case, Congress has effectively compelled a criminal investigation of a high-level appointee of the President in connection with his actions arising out of a bitter power dispute between the President and the Legislative Branch. Mr. Olson may or may not be guilty of a crime; we do not know. But we do know that the in-

vestigation of him has been commenced, not necessarily because the President or his authorized subordinates believe it is
in the interest of the United States, in the sense that it warrants
the diversion of resources from other efforts, and is worth the
cost in money and in possible damage to other governmental
interests; and not even, leaving aside those normally considered
factors, because the President or his authorized subordinates
necessarily believe that an investigation is likely to unearth a violation worth prosecuting; but only because the Attorney General cannot affirm, as Congress demands, that there are no
reasonable grounds to believe that further investigation is war-
ranted. The decisions regarding the scope of that further investigation, its duration, and, finally, whether or not prosecution
should ensue, are likewise beyond the control of the President
and his subordinates.

If to describe this case is not to decide it, the concept of a
government of separate and coordinate powers no longer has
meaning. . . .

It seems to me . . . that . . . the present statute must be [struck
down] on fundamental separation-of-powers principles if the
following question [is] answered affirmatively: . . . Does the
statute deprive the President of the United States of exclusive
control over the exercise of that power? . . .

. . . The Court does not, and could not possibly, assert that it
does not. That is indeed the whole object of the statute. . . .

. . . The case is over when the Court acknowledges, as it
must, that "[i]t is undeniable that the Act reduces the amount
of control or supervision that the Attorney General and,
through him, the President exercises over the investigation and
prosecution of a certain class of alleged criminal activity." . . . It
is not for us to determine, and we have never presumed to determine, how much of the purely executive powers of govern-

ment must be within the full control of the President. The
Constitution prescribes that they all are....

...The checks against any branch's abuse of its exclusive
powers are twofold: First, retaliation by one of the other
branch's use of its exclusive powers: Congress, for example, can
impeach the executive who willfully fails to enforce the laws;
the executive can decline to prosecute under unconstitutional
statutes, and the courts can dismiss malicious prosecutions.
Second, and ultimately, there is the political check that the people will replace those in the political branches...who are guilty
of abuse. Political pressures produced special prosecutors—for
Teapot Dome and for Watergate, for example—long before this
statute created the independent counsel.

The Court has, nonetheless, replaced the clear constitutional prescription that the executive power belongs to the President with a "balancing test." What are the standards to
determine how the balance is to be struck, that is, how much
removal of Presidential power is too much? Many countries of
the world get along with an executive that is much weaker than
ours—in fact, entirely dependent upon the continued support
of the legislature. Once we depart from the text of the Constitution, just where short of that do we stop?...Evidently, the
governing standard is to be what might be called the unfettered
wisdom of a majority of this Court, revealed to an obedient
people on a case-by-case basis. This is not only not the government of laws that the Constitution established; it is not a government of laws at all.

In my view, moreover, even as an ad hoc, standardless judgment the Court's conclusion must be wrong. Before this statute
was passed, the President, in taking action disagreeable to the
Congress, or an executive officer giving advice to the President
or testifying before Congress concerning one of those many

matters on which the two branches are from time to time at odds, could be assured that his acts and motives would be adjudged—insofar as the decision whether to conduct a criminal investigation and to prosecute is concerned—in the Executive Branch, that is, in a forum attuned to the interests and the policies of the Presidency.... It is the very object of this legislation to eliminate that assurance of a sympathetic forum. Unless it can honestly be said that there are "no reasonable grounds to believe" that further investigation is warranted, further investigation must ensue; and the conduct of the investigation, and determination of whether to prosecute, will be given to a person neither selected by nor subject to the control of the President—who will in turn assemble a staff by finding out, presumably, who is willing to put aside whatever else they are doing, for an indeterminate period of time, in order to investigate and prosecute the President or a particular named individual in his administration. The prospect is frightening... even outside the context of a bitter, interbranch political dispute. Perhaps the boldness of the President himself will not be affected—though I am not even sure of that. (How much easier it is for Congress, instead of accepting the political damage attendant to the commencement of impeachment proceedings against the President on trivial grounds—or, for that matter, how easy it is for one of the President's political foes outside of Congress—simply to trigger a debilitating criminal investigation of the Chief Executive under this law.) But as for the President's high-level assistants, who typically have no political base of support, it is as utterly unrealistic to think that they will not be intimidated by this prospect, and that their advice to him and their advocacy of his interests before a hostile Congress will not be affected, as it would be to think that the Members of Congress and their staffs would be unaffected by replacing the

Speech or Debate Clause with a similar provision. It deeply wounds the President, by substantially reducing the President's ability to protect himself and his staff. That is the whole object of the law, of course, and I cannot imagine why the Court believes it does not succeed.

Besides weakening the Presidency by reducing the zeal of his staff, it must also be obvious that the institution of the independent counsel enfeebles him more directly in his constant confrontations with Congress, by eroding his public support. Nothing is so politically effective as the ability to charge that one's opponent and his associates are not merely wrongheaded, naive, ineffective, but, in all probability, "crooks." And nothing so effectively gives an appearance of validity to such charges as a Justice Department investigation and, even better, prosecution. The present statute provides ample means for that sort of attack, assuring that massive and lengthy investigations will occur, not merely when the Justice Department in the application of its usual standards believes they are called for, but whenever it cannot be said that there are "no reasonable grounds to believe" they are called for. . . .

The purpose of the separation and equilibration of powers in general, and of the unitary Executive in particular, was not merely to assure effective government but to preserve individual freedom. Those who hold or have held offices covered by the Ethics in Government Act are entitled to that protection as much as the rest of us, and I conclude my discussion by considering the effect of the Act upon the fairness of the process they receive.

Only someone who has worked in the field of law enforcement can fully appreciate the vast power and the immense discretion that are placed in the hands of a prosecutor with respect to the objects of his investigation. Justice Robert Jackson, when he was Attorney General under President Franklin Roosevelt, described it in a memorable speech to United States Attorneys, as follows:

> There is a most important reason why the prosecutor should have, as nearly as possible, a detached and impartial view of all groups in his community. Law enforcement is not automatic. It isn't blind. One of the greatest difficulties of the position of prosecutor is that he must pick his cases, because no prosecutor can even investigate all of the cases in which he receives complaints. If the Department of Justice were to make even a pretense of reaching every probable violation of federal law, ten times its present staff will be inadequate. We know that no local police force can strictly enforce the traffic laws, or it would arrest half the driving population on any given morning. What every prosecutor is practically required to do is to select the cases for prosecution and to select those in which the offense is the most flagrant, the public harm the greatest, and the proof the most certain.
>
> If the prosecutor is obliged to choose his case, it follows that he can choose his defendants. Therein is the most dangerous power of the prosecutor: that he will pick people that he thinks he should get, rather than cases that need to be prosecuted. With the law books filled with a great assortment of crimes, a prosecutor stands a fair chance of finding at least a technical violation of some act on the part of almost anyone. In such a case, it is not a question of discovering the commission of a crime and then looking for the man who has committed it, it is a question of picking the man and then searching the law books, or putting investigators to work, to pin some offense on him. It is in this realm—in which the prosecutor picks some person whom he dislikes or desires

to embarrass, or selects some group of unpopular persons and then looks for an offense, that the greatest danger of abuse of prosecuting power lies. It is here that law enforcement becomes personal, and the real crime becomes that of being unpopular with the predominant or governing group, being attached to the wrong political views, or being personally obnoxious to or in the way of the prosecutor himself.

Under our system of government, the primary check against prosecutorial abuse is a political one. The prosecutors who exercise this awesome discretion are selected and can be removed by a President, whom the people have trusted enough to elect. Moreover, when crimes are not investigated and prosecuted fairly, nonselectively, with a reasonable sense of proportion, the President pays the cost in political damage to his administration. If federal prosecutors "pick people that [they] thin[k] [they] should get, rather than cases that need to be prosecuted," if they amass many more resources against a particular prominent individual, or against a particular class of political protesters, or against members of a particular political party, than the gravity of the alleged offenses or the record of successful prosecutions seems to warrant, the unfairness will come home to roost in the Oval Office. I leave it to the reader to recall the examples of this in recent years. That result, of course, was precisely what the Founders had in mind when they provided that all executive powers would be exercised by a single Chief Executive. As Hamilton put it, "[t]he ingredients which constitute safety in the republican sense are a due dependence on the people, and a due responsibility." [From the *Federalist Papers*, No. 70.] The President is directly dependent on the people, and since there is only one President, he is responsible. The people know whom to blame, whereas "one of the weightiest objections to a plurality in the executive . . . is that it tends to conceal faults and destroy responsibility."

That is the system of justice the rest of us are entitled to, but what of that select class consisting of present or former high-level Executive Branch officials? . . . An independent counsel is selected, and the scope of his or her authority prescribed, by a panel of judges. What if they are politically partisan, as judges have been known to be, and select a prosecutor antagonistic to the administration, or even to the particular individual who has been selected for this special treatment? There is no remedy for that, not even a political one. Judges, after all, have life tenure, and appointing a surefire enthusiastic prosecutor could hardly be considered an impeachable offense. So if there is anything wrong with the selection, there is effectively no one to blame. The independent counsel thus selected proceeds to assemble a staff. As I observed earlier, in the nature of things this has to be done by finding lawyers who are willing to lay aside their current careers for an indeterminate amount of time, to take on a job that has no prospect of permanence and little prospect for promotion. One thing is certain, however: it involves investigating and perhaps prosecuting a particular individual. Can one imagine a less equitable manner of fulfilling the executive responsibility to investigate and prosecute? What would be the reaction if, in an area not covered by this statute, the Justice Department posted a public notice inviting applicants to assist in an investigation and possible prosecution of a certain prominent person? Does this not invite what Justice Jackson described as "picking the man and then searching the law books, or putting investigators to work, to pin some offense on him"? To be sure, the investigation must relate to the area of criminal offense specified by the life-tenured judges. But that has often been (and nothing prevents it from being) very broad—and should the independent counsel or his or her staff come up with something beyond that scope, nothing prevents him or her from asking the judges to expand his or her authority or, if that does not work, referring it to the Attorney General, whereupon the whole process would recommence and, if there was "reasonable basis to believe" that further investigation was war-ranted, that new offense would be referred to the Special Division, which would in all likelihood assign it to the same independent counsel. It seems to me not conducive to fairness. But even if it were entirely evident that unfairness was in fact the result—the judges hostile to the administration, the independent counsel an old foe of the President, the staff refugees from the recently defeated administration—there would be no one accountable to the public to whom the blame could be assigned. . . .

It is, in other words, an additional advantage of the unitary Executive that it can achieve a more uniform application of the law. Perhaps that is not always achieved, but the mechanism to achieve it is there. The mini-Executive that is the independent counsel, however, operating in an area where so little is law and so much is discretion, is intentionally cut off from the unifying influence of the Justice Department, and from the perspective that multiple responsibilities provide. What would normally be regarded as a technical violation (there are no rules defining such things), may in his or her small world assume the proportions of an indictable offense. What would normally be regarded as an investigation that has reached the level of pursuing such picayune matters that it should be concluded, may to him or her be an investigation that ought to go on for another year. How frightening it must be to have your own independent counsel and staff appointed, with nothing else to do but to investigate you until investigation is no longer worthwhile—with whether it is worthwhile not depending upon what such judgments usually hinge on, competing responsibilities. And to have that counsel and staff decide, with no basis for comparison, whether what you have done is bad enough, willful enough, and provable enough, to warrant an indictment. How admirable the constitutional system that provides the means to avoid such a distortion. And how unfortunate the judicial decision that has permitted it.

The notion that every violation of law should be prosecuted, including—indeed, especially—every violation by those in high places, is an attractive one, and it would be risky to argue in an election campaign that that is not an absolutely overriding value. *Fiat justitia, ruat coelum*. Let justice be done, though the heavens may fall. The reality is, however, that it is not an absolutely overriding value, and it was with the hope that we would be able to acknowledge and apply such realities that the Constitution spared us, by life tenure, the necessity of election campaigns. I cannot imagine that there are not many thoughtful men and women in Congress who realize that the benefits of this legislation are far outweighed by its harmful effect upon our system of government, and even upon the nature of justice received by those men and women who agree to serve in the Executive Branch. But it is difficult to vote not to enact, and even more difficult to vote to repeal, a statute called, appropriately enough, the Ethics in Government Act. If Congress is controlled by the party other than the one to which the President belongs, it has little incentive to repeal it; if it is controlled by the same party, it dare not. By its shortsighted action today, I fear the Court has permanently encumbered the Republic with an institution that will do it great harm.

Worse than what it has done, however, is the manner in which it has done it. A government of laws means a government of rules. Today's decision on the basic issue of fragmentation of executive power is ungoverned by rule, and hence ungoverned by law....

The ad hoc approach to constitutional adjudication has real attraction, even apart from its work-saving potential. It is guaranteed to produce a result, in every case, that will make a majority of the Court happy with the law. The law is, by definition, precisely what the majority thinks, taking all things into account, it ought to be. I prefer to rely upon the judgment of the wise men who constructed our system, and of the people who approved it, and of two centuries of history that have shown it to be sound. Like it or not, that judgment says, quite plainly, that "[t]he executive Power shall be vested in a President of the United States."

⚜ ⚜ ⚜

We all know the consequences of the Court's decision. On some matters Justice Scalia appears to have seen the future and how it worked. During the Clinton administration, Attorney General Janet Reno appointed a special prosecutor, within the Department of Justice, to investigate allegations of presidential wrongdoing in connection with some investments in Arkansas. The prosecutor concluded that there was enough evidence to trigger the independent counsel statute, and the Attorney General asked the special court to appoint one. That court, which some Democrats later charged—as Justice Scalia predicted they would—was dominated by conservatives hostile to the president, named Kenneth Starr as independent counsel. Things spiraled out of control as Starr's investigation wandered into new areas, eventually leading to false testimony by the president to a grand jury, Starr's delivery of the evidence he compiled to the Republican-dominated House of Representatives,

Clinton's impeachment by the House and acquittal by the Senate. At least on the policy level, Justice Scalia seems to have been right.

Perhaps not, though. Contrary to Justice Scalia's prediction, Congress allowed the independent counsel statute to expire in 1999: Republicans did not like how it had been used against their friends, and Democrats agreed once they became targets. The need for someone to investigate wrongdoing by high administration officials did not disappear, and the old-fashioned method of having the attorney general name an "independent" prosecutor—on the model of Archibald Cox during Watergate —returned. It was used in the prosecution of I. Lewis "Scooter" Libby, the chief of staff for Vice President Dick Cheney. And, predictably, Republicans complained that Peter Fitzgerald, the prosecutor, went after his prey with the same single-mindedness that Justice Scalia thought was a problem with the independent counsel statute, disregarding the constraints prosecutors ordinarily operate under.

The examples of Cox and Fitzgerald cast doubt on the proposition that the independent counsel statute set up the only effective technique for going after wrongdoing high up in the executive branch. Justice Scalia pointed to the reason, as well. Presidents are politicians who worry about the political consequences of their actions. Covering up wrongdoing poses real political risks, and once the pressure is great enough the sensible thing to do is let an investigation start. At that point, as President Nixon discovered, there are further political risks in trying to control the investigation's scope. When the stench of wrongdoing is strong enough, a prosecutor from within the Department of Justice will be as independent of real presidential control as the independent counsels were.

There almost certainly were fewer investigations of executive branch wrongdoing after the independent counsel statute expired than there would have been under the statute. The statute's trigger could be pulled at a point before there would be enough political pressure on the president to appoint a special prosecutor. But the political environment differed as well. One reason there was less political pressure to investigate wrongdoing was that, for the first years after the independent counsel statute expired, we had unified government, with Republicans controlling the executive and legislative branches. If we return to an extended period of divided government, we might see more special prosecutors appointed.

The Bush administration pursued another constitutional vision described—though only in part—by Justice Scalia. This is the theory of the unitary executive, a phrase Justice Scalia used. That theory took hold fairly modestly during the Reagan administration. Conservative constitutional theorists insisted that the Constitution gave the executive branch a completely hierarchical structure: it was a pyramid with the president at the top. The president had the constitutional power—and under the clause requiring that the president "take Care that the Laws be faithfully executed," the constitutional duty—to set the policies the administration would pursue. In *Morrison,* the policies involved criminal prosecution, such as determining enforcement priorities and deciding whether pursuing a particular criminal prosecution would on balance serve the nation's interests.

In its early years, the real payoff of the "unitary executive" theory came in connection with the Reagan administration's deregulatory policies. Congress created a number of independent regulatory agencies such as the Securities and Exchange Commission, over which the president did not have direct policy control. These agencies would be unconstitutional under the "unitary executive" theory. Pro-regulatory liberals were worried about that. They should not have been. Most regulation comes from agencies that are clearly in the executive branch, such as the Environmental Protection Agency, already fitting within the unitary executive. Formally, the President controls regulatory policies announced by such agencies. President Reagan's deregulatory initiatives were limited not because he was not at the top of the administrative pyramid, but because politicians and the public would let deregulation go only so far.

The "unitary executive" theory was a defensible and perhaps even a sensible account of the way the Constitution structured the executive branch. During the administration of George W. Bush, the "unitary executive" theory morphed into something else, really having almost nothing other than the label in common with its predecessor. For some in the Bush administration, the fact that the executive branch was unitary meant not only that it was internally controlled by the president, but that in important ways the president's powers could not be controlled by statutory law at all.

The argument had two branches, corresponding to the two most important presidential powers, the commander-in-chief power and the power to take care that the laws be faithfully executed. Under the new version of the "unitary executive" theory, the president could make military decisions as commander-in-chief, and neither Congress nor the courts could limit such decisions. Perhaps that was right in connection with decisions to deploy troops to one front in a declared war instead of another, although even that is questionable. But the Bush administration's claims went farther. They went beyond the claim that Congress and the courts could not challenge the president's military decisions as commander-in-chief to the more sweeping claim that they could not even challenge the president's assertion that some decision *was* military. So, for example, if the president decided that detaining a U.S. citizen without trial as an unlawful enemy combatant aided in the prosecution of the war on terror, courts had to accept that decision and Congress could not limit the president's choices.

The "take care" power bolstered, or perhaps provided the foundation for, this expanded version of the "unitary executive" theory. According to the Bush administration, the president had the duty to take care that *all* the laws be faithfully executed. The Constitution was one of those laws, and by its own terms it was superior to mere statutes. So, if Congress passed a statute that, in the president's view, trenched on the president's constitutional powers (such as the broadly construed commander-in-chief power), the "take care" clause required that the president ignore the statute.

When push came to shove, the Bush administration was not in a strong enough political position to sustain its version of the "unitary executive" theory. It always bolstered its arguments by saying that Congress had in fact enacted statutes that authorized the president to do what he had done. The congressional Authorization for the Use of Military Force against those responsible for the September 11 attacks on the World Trade Center was the all-purpose statute on which the administration relied most often—to justify detention of U.S. citizens as enemy combatants in the face of a statute prohibiting such detentions without congressional authorization (the Supreme Court agreed with the Bush administration on that score), and to justify the adoption of a program of surveillance of international telephone calls to and (apparently) from U.S. residents in the face of a statutory ban on such surveillance.

The need for an administration in a weakened political position to look to statutes to justify its most questionable actions might ironically show that the modern "unitary executive" theory is right after all. In its essence, that theory asserts that the constraints on an administration that people think has gone off the tracks are political rather than legal. And political constraints, not legal ones, were indeed what appear—as of June 2007—to have pulled the Bush administration back.

CHAPTER 16

"Do not believe it."

Lawrence v. Texas, 2003

After gradually drifting to the right from 1973 to 1986 while Warren Burger was Chief Justice, the Supreme Court became decidedly more conservative under Chief Justice William Rehnquist, who presided over the Court from 1986 until his death in 2005. The Court's conservatism came through both in the substance of the Court's decisions and in its methods of constitutional interpretation. Although few Warren Court precedents were expressly overruled, they were increasingly confined to the precise facts the cases presented, and the Court did not extend the decisions to the limits of their logic. The Rehnquist Court also purported to shift from what some described as the freewheeling interpretive methods characteristic of the Warren Court, exemplified by the reference to "penumbras" and "emanations" in *Griswold v. Connecticut* (Chapter 14), to methods more closely tied to constitutional text and original understandings.

The Rehnquist Court might have taken the 1973 abortion decisions as a target, on both substantive and methodological grounds. And indeed the Rehnquist Court ate away at the abortion decisions around the edges. But, in 1993, the Court— with its most conservative members dissenting—reaffirmed what three justices called the "core holding" of the abortion decisions (*Planned Parenthood of Southeastern Pennsylvania v.*

Casey, 1993), and it was not until 2007, under Chief Justice John Roberts, that the Court handed down a decision with real doctrinal potential to reverse *Roe v. Wade* (*Gonzales v. Carhart,* 2007). The reason for *Roe's* persistence is reasonably clear: as the three justices put it in 1993, the decision had settled in to the nation's understanding of what the Constitution meant, and overturning it would have been quite disruptive to that understanding—not to mention how disruptive it would have been to the political system and, particularly, to the Republican Party, which would have been stretched perhaps to the breaking point by a conflict between its socially conservative "base" and more centrist voters who liked *other* aspects of the Republican platform.

There was, however, another target for social conservatism: the increasing pressure generated by gay and lesbian activists for some constitutional protection for their sexual identities. State legislatures and courts throughout the country slowly acceded to those pressures by repealing long-standing laws against voluntary same-sex sexual contact, described generically as antisodomy laws. Gay rights activists hoped to establish that antisodomy laws violated their constitutional right to privacy, but in 1986 the Supreme Court rejected that argument (*Bowers v. Hardwick,* 1986).

The gay rights movement did not give up—and neither did its opponents. After Colorado's voters amended their state's constitution by referendum, to deny "protected status" to gays and lesbians, the Supreme Court held in 1996 that the amendment violated the equal protection clause (*Romer v. Evans,* 1996). Justice Anthony Kennedy's opinion opened by quoting Justice Harlan's dissent in *Plessy v. Ferguson* (Chapter 5): "One century ago, the first Justice Harlan admonished this Court that the Constitution 'neither knows nor tolerates classes among citizens.' Unheeded then, those words now are understood to state a commitment to the law's neutrality where the rights of persons are at stake." The opinion closed with a similar rhetorical flourish: "A State cannot...deem a class of persons a stranger to its laws." Coupled with real analytic difficulties the Court overcame on its path to invalidating Colorado's amendment, these words signaled that something dramatic had happened to the Court's understanding of gay rights.

The other shoe dropped in 2003, when the Court overruled its 1986 decision and held that antisodomy laws did violate the Constitution. *Lawrence v. Texas* began when a neighbor—perhaps jealous—telephoned the police to complain that a fight was going on nearby. The report was false, but when the police arrived they discovered John Lawrence engaged in sexual activity with a partner he had just met. For some reason the Houston prosecutors decided to pursue the case using the state's antisodomy law and obtained a conviction, which the state courts affirmed. When the Supreme Court granted review, the city's lawyer was visibly uncomfortable in his attempt to defend the statute against constitutional challenge, and some observers described his argument, somewhat unfairly, as the worst they had ever seen at the Court.

Justice Kennedy once again wrote the Court's opinion, which drew upon changes in the law between 1986 and 2003 and, controversially, upon the treatment of gay rights in international human rights law. He described the activity made illegal by Texas as "one element in a personal bond that is more enduring." And, once again, his opinion ended on a high rhetorical note: the constitution's framers "knew times can blind us to certain truths and later generations can see that laws once thought necessary and proper in fact serve only to oppress. As the Constitution endures, persons in every generation can invoke its principles in their own search for greater freedom."

⚜ ⚜ ⚜

JUSTICE SCALIA, with whom THE CHIEF JUSTICE and JUS-
TICE THOMAS join, dissenting. . . .

Texas Penal Code Ann. § 21.06(a) (2003) undoubtedly im-
poses constraints on liberty. So do laws prohibiting prostitution, recreational use of heroin, and, for that matter, working
more than 60 hours per week in a bakery. But there is no right
to "liberty" under the Due Process Clause. . . . The Fourteenth
Amendment *expressly allows* States to deprive their citizens of
"liberty," so long as *"due process of law" is provided.* . . .

Our opinions applying the doctrine known as "substantive
due process" hold that the Due Process Clause prohibits States
from infringing *fundamental* liberty interests, unless the infringement is narrowly tailored to serve a compelling state
interest. We have held repeatedly, in cases the Court today does
not overrule, that *only* fundamental rights qualify for this so-
called "heightened scrutiny" protection—that is, rights which
are "'deeply rooted in this Nation's history and tradition.'" All
other liberty interests may be abridged or abrogated pursuant
to a validly enacted state law if that law is rationally related to a
legitimate state interest. . . .

I turn now to the ground on which the Court squarely rests
its holding: the contention that there is no rational basis for the
law here under attack. This proposition is so out of accord with
our jurisprudence—indeed, with the jurisprudence of *any* society we know—that it requires little discussion.

The Texas statute undeniably seeks to further the belief of
its citizens that certain forms of sexual behavior are "immoral
and unacceptable"—the same interest furthered by criminal
laws against fornication, bigamy, adultery, adult incest, bestial-
ity, and obscenity. *Bowers* held that this *was* a legitimate state
interest. The Court today reaches the opposite conclusion. The

Texas statute, it says, "furthers *no legitimate state interest* which can justify its intrusion into the personal and private life of the individual" (emphasis added).... If, as the Court asserts, the promotion of majoritarian sexual morality is not even a *legitimate* state interest, none of the above-mentioned laws can survive rational-basis review....

Today's opinion is the product of a Court, which is the product of a law-profession culture, that has largely signed on to the so-called homosexual agenda, by which I mean the agenda promoted by some homosexual activists directed at eliminating the moral opprobrium that has traditionally attached to homosexual conduct. I noted in an earlier opinion the fact that the American Association of Law Schools (to which any reputable law school *must* seek to belong) excludes from membership any school that refuses to ban from its job-interview facilities a law firm (no matter how small) that does not wish to hire as a prospective partner a person who openly engages in homosexual conduct.

One of the most revealing statements in today's opinion is the Court's grim warning that the criminalization of homosexual conduct is "an invitation to subject homosexual persons to discrimination both in the public and in the private spheres." It is clear from this that the Court has taken sides in the culture war, departing from its role of assuring, as neutral observer, that the democratic rules of engagement are observed. Many Americans do not want persons who openly engage in homosexual conduct as partners in their business, as scoutmasters for their children, as teachers in their children's schools, or as boarders in their home. They view this as protecting themselves and their families from a lifestyle that they believe to be immoral and destructive. The Court views it as "discrimination" which it is the function of our judgments to deter. So imbued is the Court with the law profession's anti-anti-homosexual culture, that it is seemingly unaware that the attitudes of that culture are not obviously "mainstream"; that in most States what the Court calls "discrimination" against those who engage in homosexual acts is perfectly legal; that proposals to ban such "discrimination" under Title VII have repeatedly been rejected by Congress; that in some cases such "discrimination" is *mandated* by federal statute, see 10 U.S.C. § 654(b)(1) (mandating discharge from the armed forces of any service member who engages in or intends to engage in homosexual acts); and that in some cases such "discrimination" is a constitutional right.

Let me be clear that I have nothing against homosexuals, or any other group, promoting their agenda through normal democratic means. Social perceptions of sexual and other morality change over time, and every group has the right to persuade its fellow citizens that its view of such matters is the best. That homosexuals have achieved some success in that enterprise is attested to by the fact that Texas is one of the few remaining States that criminalize private, consensual homosexual acts. But persuading one's fellow citizens is one thing, and imposing one's views in absence of democratic majority will is something else. I would no more *require* a State to criminalize homosexual acts—or, for that matter, display *any* moral disapprobation of them—than I would *forbid* it to do so. What Texas has chosen to do is well within the range of traditional democratic action, and its hand should not be stayed through the invention of a brand-new "constitutional right" by a Court that is impatient of democratic change. It is indeed true that "later generations can see that laws once thought necessary and proper in fact serve only to oppress"; and when that happens, later generations can repeal those laws. But it is the premise of our system that those judgments are to be made by the people, and not imposed by a governing caste that knows best.

One of the benefits of leaving regulation of this matter to

the people rather than to the courts is that the people, unlike judges, need not carry things to their logical conclusion. The people may feel that their disapprobation of homosexual conduct is strong enough to disallow homosexual marriage, but not strong enough to criminalize private homosexual acts—and may legislate accordingly. The Court today pretends that it possesses a similar freedom of action, so that we need not fear judicial imposition of homosexual marriage, as has recently occurred in Canada (in a decision that the Canadian Government has chosen not to appeal). At the end of its opinion—after having laid waste the foundations of our rational-basis jurisprudence—the Court says that the present case "does not involve whether the government must give formal recognition to any relationship that homosexual persons seek to enter." Do not believe it. More illuminating than this bald, unreasoned disclaimer is the progression of thought displayed by an earlier passage in the Court's opinion, which notes the constitutional protections afforded to "personal decisions relating to *marriage, procreation, contraception, family relationships, child rearing, and education*," and then declares that "persons in a homosexual relationship may seek autonomy for these purposes, just as heterosexual persons do." Today's opinion dismantles the structure of constitutional law that has permitted a distinction to be made between heterosexual and homosexual unions, insofar as formal recognition in marriage is concerned. If moral disapprobation of homosexual conduct is "no legitimate state interest" for purposes of proscribing that conduct; and if, as the Court coos (casting aside all pretense of neutrality), "when sexuality finds overt expression in intimate conduct with another person, the conduct can be but one element in a personal bond that is more enduring"; what justification could there possibly be for denying the benefits of marriage to homosexual couples exercising "the liberty protected by the Constitution"? Surely not the encouragement of procreation, since the sterile and the elderly are allowed to marry. This case "does not involve" the issue of homosexual marriage only if one entertains the belief that principle and logic have nothing to do with the decisions of this Court. Many will hope that, as the Court comfortingly assures us, this is so.

The matters appropriate for this Court's resolution are only three: Texas's prohibition of sodomy neither infringes a "fundamental right" (which the Court does not dispute), nor is unsupported by a rational relation to what the Constitution considers a legitimate state interest, nor denies the equal protection of the laws. I dissent.

⚜ ⚜ ⚜

On the surface, Justice Scalia's dissent is similar to Justice Black's dissent in *Griswold:* whether a state has a law against sodomy should be left to the state's voters, and the national trend toward eliminating such statutes suggests that success in Texas might not have been far off. Beneath the surface, though, differences appear. Justice Scalia's references to the "homosexual agenda" and to private discrimination against gays and lesbians make it clear that, were Justice Scalia a legislator, he would vote in favor of retaining the state's prohibition. (In a separate dissent, Justice Thomas said that as a legislator he would vote to repeal the ban.) Justice Black's dissent in *Griswold* was motivated by his constitutional theory independent of his views on the wisdom of the statute there as a matter of social policy. For Justice Scalia, in contrast, constitutional theory and policy views converge. Convergence is far more common than independence. The fact that justices regularly invoke general approaches to constitutional interpretation to uphold statutes that they think are good social policy, and invoke those same approaches to strike down statutes that they think are bad social policy, is probably the largest scandal about constitutional interpretation, mitigated only slightly by the relative handful of cases where we can be confident—sometimes because the justice says so, sometimes as a matter of our own judgment—that the approach to constitutional interpretation is operating independently of the justice's views on good social policy. Convergence is scandalous because it leads us to wonder, Why bother to ask the judges to interpret the Constitution if all they are going to do is find in the Constitution the social policies they favor? Law professor Alexander Bickel inveighed against evaluating the justices' actions based on our "moral approval of the lines," but if the judges themselves do not treat constitutional interpretation as something independent of their "moral approval" of the statutes, why should we?

The second difference between the dissents in *Griswold* and *Lawrence* is signaled by Justice Scalia's reference to the culture wars. *Griswold* pitted a constitutional theory against a social movement, and the social movement won. *Lawrence* pitted one social movement against another; the gay rights movement won, the social conservative movement lost. Why? Perhaps because, on the issue before the Court, the gay rights movement had much more popular support. Social toleration of gays had grown quite substantially in the United States in the late twentieth century, to the point where large majorities of the public—and even Republican candidates for the presidency—opposed employment discrimination against gays and lesbians.

Perhaps for that reason, Justice Scalia emphasized what he saw as the doctrinal implications of the Court's decision, and in particular its implication for the constitutionality of laws limiting the availability of marriage to heterosexual couples. As a matter of doctrine, he may be right: it is indeed quite difficult —though not impossible—to explain why barring gay marriage is consistent with the legal doctrines on which *Lawrence* rests. But, as we have repeatedly seen, doctrine does not work itself pure simply because the law is there and someone brings cases. Doctrine needs support in society, and in *Lawrence's* immediate aftermath the support for gay marriage was simply not there. Indeed, *Lawrence* and, even more, the nearly contemporaneous decision by the Massachusetts Supreme Judicial Court—finding that the state constitution required the legislature to authorize gay marriage—provoked an immediate backlash that certainly made it quite unlikely that the doctrinal implications Justice Scalia found in *Lawrence* would become constitutional law any time soon.

Other chapters in this book show that the clash between majority and dissenting positions gets resolved more in the middle to long run than in the short run, and *Lawrence* is too recent for us to know what it will ultimately mean. Yet, it may be worth observing that by 2007 support for civil unions apparently had become the centrist position on marriage: no to gay marriage, but no as well to restricting all of the legal benefits of marriage to heterosexual couples. As in *Griswold,* the Court may have observed social changes happening around it, and tried to give some *constitutional* basis for claims that were already succeeding politically.

CONCLUSION

The fate of a dissent lies in the hands of history. Justice McReynolds's dissent in *Jones & Laughlin* (Chapter 8) remains "wrong" because constitutional law has not yet come around to the position he took. Justice Scalia's dissents *might* be prescient, but he is not yet a great dissenter because we do not know how the story will turn out.

This perspective raises questions about the status of constitutional law as *law*. In case after case in this book, we have seen how courts fit into the larger political system. Nor is this merely an artifact of the choices I have made in selecting the dissents presented here. As I noted in the Introduction, I chose cases where the dissents illuminated a reasonably wide range of issues drawn from the history of constitutional law. Replacing one case with another—*Griswold v. Connecticut* with *Roe v. Wade,* for example—would not change the overall picture. Nor indeed would coming up with an entirely different set of cases, at least where the choices were still dictated by a desire to illustrate constitutional law and history generally. And I suspect that the same picture would have emerged even if I had used a different selection principle, such as "Choose dissents that rely almost entirely on the proposition that the only proper way to interpret the Constitution is 'originalist,' referring to the Constitution's words as they were understood when they were placed in the Constitution."

Dissents are vindicated because the social, economic, or political environment changes. Or they seem increasingly out of touch with reality for precisely the same reason. As political scientist Robert Dahl put it in 1957, the courts rarely hold out for long against a sustained movement in national politics—and indeed it would be surprising to find a stable political system in which one component was regularly at odds with others.

Does that mean that constitutional law is merely politics in disguise? Here we should distinguish between the perspective of lawyers and judges on the one hand, and that of ordinary citizens on the other. For lawyers arguing constitutional cases, knowing that constitutional law tracks political and social developments is decidedly unhelpful. That knowledge seems to make *legal* arguments irrelevant. A lawyer cannot stand up in front of the nine justices and say, "I should win because society is moving in my direction." Nor do judges regularly ask whether the constitutional interpretation they favor fits well with political and social trends. Sometimes legal doctrine itself makes social trends relevant, but not across a wide range of constitutional issues. In general, judges look to law—the Constitution's text, precedents, principles they see in the text and history—to guide their decisions.

For lawyers and judges, law has to matter. And it can. At any moment, a judge cannot really know where society and politics are going. The path forward has many forks. A judge self-consciously aiming to predict the future may wander on to a dead end. Better, it seems, to decide by treating the legal materials as the only things to worry about. Even more, sometimes, a judge's legal interpretation may help nudge politics and social change on to a new path, slightly different from the one that the society would have taken had the judge interpreted the

Constitution differently. Lawyers and judges tend to celebrate *Brown v. Board of Education* in such terms, although Justice Jackson's observation that the ruling was in some sense inevitable cautions against giving too much credit to the Court for what happened later. Still, judges' inability to foresee the future clearly and their modest influence on the future gives the Constitution some role as law in what they do.

For ordinary citizens, I think, the perspective is different. Not bound up in the enterprise of making constitutional law in court, ordinary citizens need not worry about the law's technicalities. Popular constitutionalism asserts that we each are entitled to develop our own constitutional vision, without much regard to what the courts have said. As citizens, we can properly see the constitutional law handed down by the courts as a reflection of social and political developments. And, seeing it that way helps us understand our role as citizens in the constitutional order. We, not the courts, are the ultimate sources of constitutional law. How we implement our constitutional visions in social movements and through political action will eventually determine what the courts say the Constitution means. As citizens we should think hard about the Constitution, informed by the courts—but also informed by what dissenters have to say to us.

SOURCES AND ADDITIONAL READINGS

I have included below the proper citations for each chapter's Supreme Court case as well as a book title or two for each case that may prove useful for additional reading.

CHAPTER 1

Marbury v. Madison, 5 U.S. (1 Cranch) 137 (1803) with dissenting opinion from *Eakin v. Raub,* 12 Sergeant & Rawle 330 (1825) (Pennsylvania Supreme Court).

Ackerman, Bruce. *The Failure of the Founding Fathers: Jefferson, Marshall, and the Rise of Presidential Democracy.* (Cambridge, MA: Harvard University Press, 2005.)

Nelson, William. *Marbury v. Madison: The Origins and Legacy of Judicial Review.* (Lawrence: University Press of Kansas, 2000.)

CHAPTER 2

McCulloch v. Maryland, 17 U.S. (4 Wheat.) 316 (1819), with dissent in form of a veto message found in Andrew Johnson, James D. Richardson, ed., *Messages and Papers of the Presidents,* vol. 2 (New York: Bureau of National Literature, 1917.)

Killenbeck, Mark. *McCulloch v. Maryland: Securing a Nation.* (Lawrence: University Press of Kansas, 2006.)

Magliocca, Gerard N. *Andrew Jackson and the Constitution: The Rise and Fall of Constitutional Regimes.* (Lawrence: University Press of Kansas, 2007.)

CHAPTER 3

Dred Scott v. Sanford, 60 U.S. (19 How.) 393 (1857)

Fehrenbacher, Don. *The Dred Scott Case: Its Significance in American Law and Politics.* (New York: Oxford University Press, 1978.)

Graber, Mark. *Dred Scott and the Problem of Constitutional Evil.* (Cambridge: Cambridge University Press, 2006.)

CHAPTER 4

The *Civil Rights Cases,* 109 U.S. 3 (1883)

Brandwein, Pamela. "The Civil Rights Cases and the Lost Language of State Neglect." In *The Supreme Court in American Political Development,* edited by Ronald Kahn and Ken Kersch. (Lawrence: University Press of Kansas, 2006.)

CHAPTER 5

Plessy v. Ferguson, 163 U.S. 537 (1896)

Lofgren, Charles. *The Plessy Case: A Legal-Historical Interpretation.* (New York: Oxford University Press USA, 1988.)

CHAPTER 6

Lochner v. New York, 198 U.S. 45 (1905)

Bernstein, David. "The Story of Lochner v. New York: Impediment to the Growth of the Regulatory State." In *Constitutional Law Stories,* edited by Michael Dorf. (New York: Foundation Press, 2004.)

Kens, Paul. *Lochner v. New York: Economic Regulation on Trial.* (Lawrence: University Press of Kansas, 1998.)

CHAPTER 7

Whitney v. California, 274 U.S. 357 (1927)

Skover, David, and Ronald Collins. "Curious Concurrence: Justice Brandeis' Vote in Whitney v. California." *Supreme Court Review* 2005 (2006): 333.

Stone, Geoffrey. *Perilous Times: Free Speech in Wartime from the Sedition Act of 1798 to the War on Terrorism.* (New York: W. W. Norton, 2004.)

CHAPTER 8

National Labor Relations Board v. Jones & Laughlin Steel Corp., 301 U.S. 1 (1937)

Cushman, Barry. *Rethinking the New Deal Court: The Structure of a Constitutional Revolution.* (New York: Oxford University Press USA, 1998.)

Jackson, Robert H. *The Struggle for Judicial Supremacy: A Study of a Crisis in American Power Politics.* (New York: Knopf, 1941.)

CHAPTER 9

Korematsu v. United States, 323 U.S. 214 (1944)

Daniels, Peter. *Prisoners Without Trial: Japanese Americans in World War II.* (New York: Hill & Wang, 1993.)

Irons, Peter. *Justice at War: The Story of the Japanese-American Internment Cases.* (Berkeley: University of California Press, 1993.)

CHAPTER 10

Goesaert v. Cleary, 335 U.S. 464 (1948)

Strum, Phillipa. *Women in the Barracks: The VMI Case and Equal Rights.* (Lawrence: University Press of Kansas, 2002.)

CHAPTER 11

Brown v. Board of Education, 347 U.S. 483 (1954), with dissent in the form of a draft opinion from the Papers of Robert H. Jackson, Manuscript Division, Library of Congress, box 184.

Klarman, Michael. *Brown v. Board of Education and the Civil Rights Movement.* (New York: Oxford University Press USA, 2007.)

Tushnet, Mark. *Making Civil Rights Law: Thurgood Marshall and the Supreme Court, 1936–1961.* (New York: Oxford University Press USA, 1994.)

CHAPTER 12

Baker v. Carr, 369 U.S. 186 (1962)

Neal, Phil C. "Baker v. Carr: Politics in Search of Law." *Supreme Court Review* 1962 (1962): 252–327.

Yarbrough, Tinsley. *Race and Redistricting: The Shaw-Cromartie Cases.* (Lawrence: University Press of Kansas, 2002.)

CHAPTER 13

Abington School District v. Schempp, 374 U.S. 203 (1963)

Dierenfield, Bruce. *The Battle Over School Prayer: How Engel v. Vitale Changed America.* (Lawrence: University Press of Kansas, 2007.)

Solomon, Stephen. *Ellery's Protest: How One Young Man Defied Tradition and Sparked the Battle over School Prayer.* (Ann Arbor: University of Michigan Press, 2007.)

CHAPTER 14

Griswold v. Connecticut, 381 U.S. 479 (1965)

Garrow, David. *Liberty and Sexuality: The Right to Privacy and the Making of Roe v. Wade.* (Berkeley: University of California Press, 1998.)

Johnson, John W. *Griswold v. Connecticut: Birth Control and the Constitutional Right of Privacy.* (Lawrence: University Press of Kansas, 2005.)

CHAPTER 15

Morrison v. Olson, 487 U.S. 654 (1988)

Harriger, Katy. *The Special Prosecutor in American Politics.* (Lawrence: University Press of Kansas, 2000.)

CHAPTER 16

Lawrence v. Texas, 539 U.S. 558 (2003)

Carpenter, Dale. "The Unknown Past of *Lawrence v. Texas.*" *Michigan Law Review* 102 (2004): 1464.

Murdoch, Joyce, and Deb Price. *Courting Justice: Gay Men and Lesbians v. the Supreme Court.* (New York: Basic Books, 2001.)